try hard

One Man's Goal in Regaining Lost Dreams

By R. Keith Simpson

Edited by Ada Mattox

ISBN: 1-4392-0134-X
ISBN-13: 9781439201343

Visit www.booksurge.com to order additional copies.

FOREWORD

I can still see Keith on that crisp November morning. Tall and slender, he entered my classroom dressed in jeans, a white shirt, and a sky-blue pullover sweater that perfectly matched the color of his eyes. His brown wavy hair was neatly combed, and my nose detected a whiff of aftershave even though there was not a whisker to be found on his fourteen-year-old face. He was laughing and making jokes, modestly accepting the praise and attention that were his on this morning after he had led the Junior Varsity basketball team to victory the night before. Oh, he was proud of himself; I could tell by his slight swagger and the care with which he had dressed, but he was doing his best to hide it.

I could see the promise in him that morning as he came into homeroom. Success surrounded him. He was good-looking with a certain boyish handsomeness, intelligent without being bookish, and athletically gifted with a self-deprecating humor—he seemed to have it all, and it was only going to get better. On that sunny morning, the world lay before him, and I was astounded by the enormity of the potential I saw in him. It was as if I were seeing him for the first time. It was one of those moments that made me glad to be a teacher, glad to be a part of this kid's life, glad for the promise of youth.

That was two months before the car accident that threw him headfirst through the passenger windshield and forever changed his life. I went to see him in the hospital. Since he was in Intensive Care, I could see him for only a moment. That was enough—enough to see that his handsome face was swollen and bruised and cut, enough to see that he could not move his right side or talk very well because of the swelling in his brain.

Oh, the doctors tried to be optimistic. "With therapy you'll improve," they said. That was true, but what they failed to say was that he would never be the way he had been. But we knew it and he knew it. And he never was.

Physically, he made progress, but emotionally he never did. My relationship with him continued as I became his home-bound tutor. We managed to get him through his freshman year, but his heart was not in it, and we both knew it. The future was bleak and uncertain, and he couldn't face it.

His father, broken over the changes in his only son, mourned Keith as if he were dead and turned to alcohol. His mother tried to "make it up" to Keith by spoiling him and letting him do whatever he wanted.

The next year Keith quit school and began to spend his insurance settlement. The year after that he enrolled in a private Christian school, and I tutored him again. He was now a bitter, cynical young man, angry with God, angry with everyone. He dropped out of that school too, and a year or so later, I helped him study for the GED exam, which he easily passed. He continued to spend his money on new cars and trucks which he recklessly tore up, expensive hobbies, and anything else which struck his fancy.

Twelve years after the accident, I still saw him occasionally, and he always greeted me warmly, but conversation was awkward for us. I suppose it was still painful for him to talk about his life before the accident, and his life since then did not make for small talk.

Once during that period, I saw Keith standing in front of Super X, waiting for a ride. He had wrecked his latest truck and confided that he had become addicted to alcohol and other drugs he had sought out to treat the pain in his injured back. His attempts to break the habit were not meeting with success. Gaunt and stooped with his shaggy beard shot through with gray, he looked much older than his twenty-six years.

I looked at him that day and remembered that golden boy of fourteen in the blue sweater, the boy who laughed and teased as he stood with the world before him on that November morning some twelve years before. I had always believed the axiom that God never sends a burden greater than one can bear. I no longer believed it. Whether or not God had sent it or simply allowed it to happen, it was a burden greater than Keith could manage. As we parted, I hugged him and then quickly turned and left before he could see the tears in my eyes—tears for what might have been, and tears for what was.

Christie Hardbarger

1991

CHAPTER I
Humble Beginnings

My early life was happy and carefree with no hint of the tragedy and struggles that were to follow. On an otherwise uneventful day, I was born to Ronald and Dreama Simpson in the Chesapeake and Ohio Hospital in Clifton Forge, Virginia. The early memories I chose to share came to me in tiny flashes attached to my age or my grade in school. The first glimmer of my extreme independence and the path I was to follow came when I was about two years old and was staying all day with my grandmother and grandfather. I cannot remember the details, but my grandfather told me that he knew then that I liked to hike. I went alone for a long walk, about a mile or so. Now, granted, I was only two years old, but I was walking home. My granddad rescued me before anyone else realized I was missing.

When I turned four, I got my first bike, a birthday gift from my parents. It was red with training wheels. I jumped on it right away and started to ride around and around in my basement. I was having a great time until I crashed into a cement wall and tore my right ear. Dad came over and saw that my ear was bleeding and rushed me to the hospital where I got four stitches. Also, in that year of "firsts," my dad took me fishing in a boat on the Cowpasture River. I was so excited, and from that point on, fishing was an important part of my life. I enjoyed also the outdoor times when people would come from everywhere to meet at my grandparents' home where we played softball, made apple butter, butchered hogs, and–my favorite thing–made ice cream. I became aware of my very close-knit family, and I wished everybody could be like that.

By the time I was five, I thought my dad was Superman. He had a horse named Fanny that was about two years old but had never been ridden. My dad trained it. He was an exceptional man and still is. We had two other horses whose names I don't remember, maybe because I don't want to. One was a big black mare with a white mane. One day when Mom was watching me ride, I rode close to her, and the mare threw me off, but Mom caught me in midair. I guess God was helping me even then. We also had a brown pony with a black mane. It was wild! I rode it one day and thought I had it under control. Then it started running really fast and began bucking. I came off the pony and was shaken up for a while. I had found one of the few things I did not like to do.

By this time I had established my love of the out-of-doors. The house I lived in at the time was surrounded by a grove of immense oak and hickory trees and had a creek running beside it. My father owned about fifteen acres; it was a nice place to grow up. That summer my family went to the beach and camped, using our fold-out camper. I liked to stay by myself, so I made a little hut in the woods out of sticks which I covered with a sheet like the tents my mom used to make for me in our house by putting sheets over the furniture. After each meal I would go there. Everything was going well until my little sister found my retreat and reported to Mom that I had taken her sheet and was using it in the woods. Paige was a big tattletale at the time.

At the traditional age of six, I went to school. I immediately liked school, especially recess. When I played kickball, I kicked the ball farther than anybody else. One day at play period, my classmates and I were all outside, and I was swinging and having a great time. Then I looked down below me, and there was a snake that I thought was a rattlesnake because of the markings. I was really frightened, but I kept on swinging. Ms. Peters came over with a stick and removed the snake. She said it was a pine snake, but for about a year I still thought it was a rattlesnake.

When I went into second grade, I was outside one day dusting erasers when a seventh-grade boy came out and pulled a pencil on me, acting like he was going to stab me with it. I couldn't tell exactly what he was holding until later because I was running so fast. That's when I first knew I could run. In third grade I painted a picture of a cardinal, the most wonderful thing I'd ever done in my life. It was a big painting that I still have in my mom's house. I also started playing football and basketball which Dad had played with me ever since I was about two. The year I played halfback in B Team football, we won the championship. In basketball I played guard. I remember one game that we were losing by one point, and I had a chance to score from under the basket, using a hook shot my dad had been teaching me for a long time. I threw the ball up and missed. That blunder stayed on my mind for about an hour. Things like that didn't bother me that much when I was young.

When I was nine, Edwin White, my pastor's son, took me canoeing on the Cowpasture River. I did fine until we came to Peters' Rapids. Although Edwin did his best to convince me that we could get through the rapids, I did not want to go, so I got out and walked. When Edwin came and picked me up, I knew that, even though I was scared, one day I would own a canoe.

In fifth grade I was elected to the Student Council Association (SCA), and I remember distinctly that I was the secretary. At the second meeting, the president called the meeting to order. Then he asked me about the minutes of the last meeting, and I said the last meeting lasted 17 and 1/2 minutes. Thinking I had misunderstood, he asked me again, and I repeated that the last meeting had lasted 17 and 1/2 minutes. The members of the SCA started laughing, and I did not know why. Then one of the teachers explained that keeping the minutes meant recording what had happened in the last meeting. I was embarrassed for a while but got over that too.

That was the first year I ever stood up for myself. Two boys were trying to take my lunch money from me. They had been doing this for quite a while. But one day I stood up against them and told them, "If you ever take money from me again, I will hurt you." That's the last time that I had trouble with them or anybody else who might want to pick on me.

One day some friends and I went tubing on the Cowpasture River from Griffith's Knob to my grandmother's property about four miles downstream. The falls were directly in our path. When we got there, I stopped to watch everyone else go down. There was a gully about four feet deep and three feet wide with rocks along it coming down through the falls. When Rodney, my eleven-year-old cousin, came over the falls, I was not looking, so I don't know exactly what happened, but when I saw him, he had fallen out of the tube and was in the gully doing cartwheels under the water. I was standing on the bank wondering what to do; then I got the giggles and couldn't stop laughing. He finally stopped turning flips and got out of the river. He assured me he was okay. For children of our age, that was a very hair-raising experience for both Rodney and me.

When I moved up to the next grade, I had Miss McGuire. She was a good teacher who liked Virginia Tech and the New York Yankees. She used to give us a lick on the hand with a paddle with holes in it when we did anything wrong. One day I had a confrontation with a boy who said he was going to beat me up. I pushed him, and he pushed me back. Miss

McGuire walked in. She gave him a lick but not me. She gave everybody in the class a lick that year but me. Yes, she was a sports fanatic. The other kids in the class thought I escaped the lick because the teacher thought I was good in sports.

That summer I went water skiing on Smith Mountain Lake with my dad and an older man we met at the lake. Our new acquaintance told me to start out on two skis and then kick off one. I did what he said. I was skiing on two and got brave and kicked off one. For a long time after that, I used only one ski. I think people can do anything if they try. Also, I guess I have some God-given talent.

One night Dad, my friend Tony, and I went fishing in the Cowpasture. We started out when it was dusky dark; it was a new experience for me. We were using black Tiny Torpedoes as top-water lure and were catching fish as soon as we dropped our lines in the water. I was a little afraid as darkness came on, but my dad being with me helped restore calm. After about an hour of fishing, something dropped from a tree into the water. Dad assured me it was probably a branch. After two more objects dropped from the trees, Dad took out his flashlight to see what was going on. The flashlight illuminated a snake, so we knew that was what we had been hearing. They continued to drop, coming closer and closer to the boat. This went on for about twenty minutes, and I was scared almost to death. I wanted off the water, but we finished the trip, put the boat on the truck, and took Tony home. We had a big fish fry the next day using the multitude of fish we had caught. We figured the snakes were mating and having a good old time.

When I was in seventh grade, I played football and basketball and was really good at both. I fell in love that year–puppy love–with a girl named Rita who gave me my first French kiss. My team did pretty well in football and won the championship in basketball. I was even named May Day king, and Rita was my queen. It was another good year in a succession I thought would never end.

My daredevil spirit really emerged one winter day when I was twelve and snows were deep. I went out to the garage, got a piece of paneling, and cut it about six feet long and a foot wide. I decided to get on a ridge near our house and try surfing down the mountain. Because I had good balance, I was able to stand up on the board and surf all the way, a distance of about a quarter of a mile almost straight down to the river. The site was perfect, an old pasture on the side of a ridge that had no trees or fences blocking my path. After my initial success, I went down about fifteen more times until my board broke. If I had just known about snowboarding, I could have marketed my invention and become a multimillionaire. Oh well, that's the way life goes!

At about the same time, I became infatuated with auto racing. My family lived up on a hill in Nicelytown, outside Clifton Forge, Virginia. Every Saturday night I used to hear cars revving up their engines, sounding like they were racing on the mile of straight stretch just below my house on Route

42. One night I decided to go to see what was happening. In order to do this, I had to sneak out my window which had a fifteen-foot drop to the ground. It was easy getting out, but it was hard getting back! Once on the ground, I walked down to a cliff overlooking the main road. I liked cars, so I was excited to see a full-fledged drag race going on in the middle of the night on a primary state road. An old 1967 Chevelle Malibu was the top car. It would get up to speeds of 160-170 miles an hour and would fly down that road. Because it was dark up on the hill where I sat, nobody ever knew I was there. I returned several more times before the summer was over and never got caught.

Back in the days when it was legal to ride motorcycles on trails in wooded areas, my friends and I had a motorcycle dirt bike gang called the Forty-Two Crew. We had about twenty members. I can remember vividly what happened once while we were eating the lunches that we had carried in our bike packs. One of our group went over a jump that was about twenty-five feet behind us. He was riding a Honda Trail 90 and pulled up too much on the handle bars. He did a complete back flip and landed upright on his wheels. After a few feet, he became so scared about what he had done that he turned the bike over. For some reason, he never went riding with us again.

One time I went riding with a man called Snake Doctor. We went up beside the C & O railroad track near my house to a place where old ties were discarded. Snake Doctor suggested that I turn over some of the ties. Being young and inexperienced, I did what he asked. Under the third tie I turned over was a big copperhead. I started to run but looked back to see what my friend was doing. He pulled something from the side of his motorcycle that I thought was a gun. It turned out to be a pair of tongs that he used to catch the snake and put it in a bag. He took it home to add to the collection in his basement. I rode many times with him again, but I never again turned over anything else that might have a snake under it.

In my eighth grade year, I started high school. I did not play football that year because I didn't like the coach, but I played basketball and really liked it. I was taking college preparatory courses, hoping to go to the University of Virginia. That was an attainable dream, for I was doing well academically as well as athletically.

Ninth grade was one the best years of my life. I played basketball and was one of the leading scorers. I could beat guys who were seniors because I was quick and smooth in my movements on the court. I could also shoot with consistent accuracy. My dad for years had supervised while I shot a hundred foul shots each day. He had drilled me in shooting left-handed and right-handed lay-ups until I felt I was ambidextrous. I was playing quarterback on the junior varsity football team and threw a touchdown pass in every game except in the one game which we lost. The varsity coach told me that I would be quarterbacking the next year, and Mr. Higgins, a coach at a rival school in Clifton Forge, said that his team was scared of me because I could both run and pass the ball.

There was one special girl at that time named Donna. She was extremely smart and beautiful, and I wanted to ask her out but was afraid to. We had classes together and talked before and after school. I was sure that when the right time came, I would ask her to go to the movies with me, and she would say yes. I had the world by the tail.

Then the unthinkable happened.

CHAPTER II
The Downhill Turn

After a basketball game one night when I was fourteen years old, I disobeyed my parents who had told me to ride home with them; instead I went with my cousin to the Holiday Inn to pick up some friends. On this cold December night, we were driving along having a good time listening to the radio in a Toyota my cousin had borrowed for the evening. As we were traveling about 65 miles an hour around a 25 mile-an-hour curve, the world suddenly came tumbling down on me. With the excessive speed, the driver lost control of the car and hit a rock wall on the passenger side. He was knocked out, but I was still conscious. I got out of the car, not knowing what was wrong with me, but my head was scalped, my jaw was broken in four places, and my cheekbone was broken. I walked back to a car that had stopped behind us to get some help from the girls who were friends of ours. One girl looked at me and vomited; I couldn't understand why until I felt my head. All I felt was the interior of my scalp. Then Miss Carter, a teacher from my school, drove up. She stood tall in the crisis, put my scalp back on my head, and took care of me.

An ambulance arrived about ten minutes later and took me to Alleghany Regional Hospital. The medical staff put bandages on my head and shipped me to Roanoke Memorial, fifty miles away. As soon as I arrived there, I went into surgery where two doctors fixed my head and two of the broken bones in my jaw before sending me to the recovery room and then to the Intensive Care Unit (ICU). The next morning I was drinking a cup of juice and passed out. The doctors couldn't figure out why then but later, after a series of tests, they discovered I had suffered a stroke. My head being swollen to the size of a watermelon had made diagnosis difficult. I was out for five hours before a surgeon operated on the left side of my neck at which time the right side of my body became paralyzed.

I have no memory of the people who came to see me the first two weeks, for my doctors wanted to keep me sedated. My parents told me later that the Alleghany High School basketball team came to see me and signed a basketball and a poster for me. On another occasion, a whole busload of students came to see me, but I didn't respond to them either. A total of 500-700 people visited me during that time, but I have no recollection of any of them. My friends reported later that many students would go to the auditorium daily to pray for me.

I spent three months in the hospital, a true nightmare which I can remember like it was yesterday. They stuck me in my right side with needles. I could not feel them, but after a week, the feeling in my right leg and right arm began coming back. I had been taking so many drugs that I had not realized before that I was paralyzed on the right side, and half of my face continued to be numb also. My muscles, in a matter of days, had shrunk to practically nothing. Physical therapists worked intensely on me for about three months. At first I thought my leg and arm would never move again, but I eventually regained some use of them. After being in the hospital three months, I got 5 percent of the use of my arm back and 10 percent of the use of my leg. I wanted so much to regain the strength in my arm and leg. I thought, "Who did this thing to me? I know it wasn't God. Then again, he sees all and knows the future. Is there a plan behind all this?"

After the swelling in my head went down, another x-ray showed my jaw was broken in two more places. This time the surgeon had to put in wires. This operation was so painful that I kept thinking something must be wrong, but the operation was successful. A dentist came up to my room one night and started moving my teeth around; that was a painful thing. In fact, that was the most pain I went through in the hospital. Because my jaws were wired together, I lived on milkshakes for three months and lost thirty-seven pounds.

I left the hospital with my jaws still wired together, but the wires were removed after a week. However, it was about a month before I could chew, for the muscles in my jaws had to stretch. I had to start off with soft foods that had been processed in a blender. I was glad to have even that much to make me feel that I was actually eating again. I also had to learn to talk and to tie my shoes with one hand. This procedure was very awkward, for I had to rely on my left hand, and I am right handed. I walked with the help of a cane.

My family and friends welcomed me home with open arms. The day I got back, my dad and some of my friends were playing basketball. I felt so bad watching them through the window that I cried. I kept thinking that three-and-a-half months ago I was excelling in a variety of sports, and now I felt helpless because I could not participate. After all I had come through to get well, I began to feel that life was over if I could not resume my role as an athlete.

After three weeks, I returned to school, but adjusting to my new way of life was too stressful. I could not talk. I would be late for classes because I could not walk fast enough. The main frustration was seeing my friends doing all the things I used to do. It was a really hard experience, so I quit after about a week.

Until this time I had been looking up; now everything seemed to fall apart. I was fifteen years old and had to find some way to put the pieces back together. The answer came in riding my Huffy ten-speed bike. Every morning someone at my home would help me get on the bike and help me take off. Then I would ride seven miles to the Ponderosa Truck Stop where I would rest. When I was ready, some friends who worked there or who waited there for me would help me prepare for my homeward journey. In the two months that I did this, I never wrecked. By this time, I was strong enough to ride the bike without help, but my right arm and right leg were still very weak. Mom worried that I would lose control and run into a car or that a car would hit me.

When summer came, I went back to Camp Accovac, a Christian camp in Millboro, as I had many years before. I had to have something in my life to cheer me up, and God was it. Somehow I expected the camp experience to be as it had always been, but it was not. Other campers stared at me because of my disabilities. After all, they were teenagers and unaccustomed to seeing another person their age with scars on his head, garbled speech, and little use of one arm and leg. I was attempting to play basketball but had to shoot from close under the basket using my left hand only when I had been a right-handed player. It was very hard, but I constantly tried to do what I couldn't do. After two weeks at camp, I was awarded the trophy for being the most athletic participant. I felt closer to God and felt he had allowed me to qualify for this honor.

All my life I have loved fishing, and there had to be some way for me to continue with this pastime. I found a pole with a long butt end. Sitting on the bank of the Cowpasture River for hours at a time, I would put the butt end of the pole between my legs and reel with my left hand. I did this for about three months until my right hand had enough strength to hold the pole in place by simply laying it on top of the pole as I reeled. I caught many a fish that summer and felt wonderful about being able to fish again.

The December I was fifteen, I started back to school but still did not like it. I began to want to ice skate as I had every winter since I was seven. One favorite skating spot for my friends and me was a place called Coleman's Tunnel. In 1919 the railroad had run through the tunnel, but that route had been closed off a long time ago, leaving a portion of the river that formed a big pond. The surface was smooth, and the ice was so clear that I could see bass and perch frozen into the ice below. Usually, it was very safe because it was the coldest place in Alleghany County. I had a pair of hockey skates which I had friends tie tight for me. By then I had 40 percent use of my leg and 15 percent use of my arm. I did most of the pushing off with my left leg. I fell a few times when I first started skating, but I continued to try. Sometimes a group of us would go at night and build a big bonfire. Although I was having a good time, the frustration of my limitations did not go away.

One day six friends and I were playing hockey and having a great time. After the game we all went skating around the pond. In one area there was an underground spring with temperatures around fifty degrees all year around. Unaware that it was there, I skated over the spring. All of a sudden the ice broke, and I went into the water. Fortunately, my foot hit a log that was wedged in the bottom of the pond, so my head stayed above the water. I yelled for my friends to help me, but the ice was too thin for them to get to me. A boy on the bank heard me calling for help and got a pole about twenty feet long. He lay on solid ice and stretched the pole out to my good hand. I grabbed it, and he pulled me in. All my friends walked with me the mile we had to go to my grandma's house. My clothes were frozen stiff and, unbelievably, kept me warm much like being in an igloo. Once again, God had been with me.

I began thinking about God, and soon after I turned sixteen, I made a profession of faith and decided to be baptized. My pastor, Doug Moore, took me out into the Cowpasture River that runs beside Mary Deed's property and immersed me and two other people. I could feel the Holy Spirit come over me; it was one of the best days of my life. For a time after that, I went to church, prayed, read my bible, and lived the Christian life.

It was during this period, on a winter day in January 1981, that Lone Star Advent Christian Church had planned a trip to North Carolina for twenty-five members of the youth group. We had a good time going down, but the bus driver drove so fast that he scared everybody, even me. When we arrived at our destination, it was bitterly cold. Taking into account the wind chill factor, the temperature on Mt. Mitchell, the tallest mountain on the East Coast, was an unbelievable 111 degrees below zero. We had planned to ski, but we were not sure we wanted to go up on the slopes when it was so cold. Finally, we decided to go anyway. Most of us had never skied before in our lives.

When we got to the ski area, the temperature was 56 degrees below zero. It was so cold that all exposed skin froze. Roger Daniels and I were skiing on the kiddy slopes, and we were dressed warmly. Then we decided to go to the intermediate slope. Roger did fine coming down the hill, but I didn't do that well; I wrecked. I lost my toboggan, my ski goggles, and my gloves. By the time I made it to the ski lodge and was taken to the rescue area, frostbite had set in on my right wrist. The paramedics bandaged me up and sent me on my way. I spent the rest of the evening by the fire in the great room. About 10:00 p.m. we got on the bus and went back to the cabins where we were staying.

There was no heat in the cabins, and all the water had frozen up, so we were in a predicament that we weren't sure how to get out of. We prayed for God's help, however, and found a way to work through our problem. First, we put on all the warm clothes we had. Then we all huddled together so that our collective body heat kept us warm. Every so often, the people on the outside were allowed to switch with those closer to the middle to take better advantage of the heat. We were really comfortable; however, don't send me travel folders about trips to Antarctica, for I think I have already been there and don't want to go back! We didn't go back to the mountains of North Carolina in the winter again either. It was a good learning experience to see how much cold the body could take, but I have a scar to remind me of how dangerous cold weather can be.

CHAPTER III
Depression Deepens

Two years after the accident, my doctor said I needed counseling. I thought he was full of mud; however, I was drinking every day, coming in at all hours of the night, wasted and tormented. Some evenings I would fall out of the truck onto the ground. My mom and dad would listen for me to come in, and one of them would come out to see if I was all right. There were many nights during this time that I despaired and hated the person I had become with no purpose in life. I could not do anything I used to do, I had no friends but my drinking buddies, and my popularity with the girls had seriously declined. I was a tortured wreck. My mom and dad talked me through these times and tried to calm me, relieving each other every hour. Eventually, I would go to bed and sleep it off, and all would be fine for a week or two. Then the cycle would repeat itself. Since I refused professional help, my parents became my counselors. They feared for my life.

About the time I turned seventeen, I hit the depths of my depression. I had no use of my right arm and had to use splints on my right leg in order to walk at all. I watched all my friends playing basketball and football while I sat useless on the sidelines, thinking I could play the same way I used to play, but I couldn't. Once I decided to go out for football anyway. When I went to get the physical, the doctor said I couldn't play because I was handicapped. I can't tell you how horrible that comment made me feel.

Depression really set in. I turned from God and went to the bottle for relief. Drinking made me forget my frustrations for a brief time, but then reality would return and I would drink again or use drugs. About this time I got a little bit of money from my accident, so I bought a new truck, got my driver's license, and did an awful lot of partying. There had been a time when I had everything going for me, and suddenly it had been taken away. I had to do something to help me forget.

Drinking finally led me to thoughts of suicide, and I tried four times unsuccessfully to end my life. God was watching out for me during these and many other episodes in my life, such as the nine wrecks I had while drinking. My depression finally got so bad that I took a length of hose and went four-wheeling to a place called Nowhere. I thought I had had enough of this world of not being able to play football, not being able to play basketball, and not getting the type of women I wanted. I hated myself and wondered what had happened to all the friends I used to have. My life was not supposed to be like this; it was supposed to be vastly different. During my early years I had known that I was going to play professional ball. Too many coaches had told me I had the talent for me not to believe in a bright future. Now, four years after the accident, at age eighteen I was experiencing trouble walking, talking, and riding a bike. I felt cheated, knowing I would never play college or professional sports, or have a decent job, a wife, children, and all those other dreams that had been laid before me. My drinking definitely compounded my depression. Now at Nowhere, I put the hose on the muffler of my truck and stuck the other end in my truck with the windows rolled up to hold in all the fumes. I started the motor, turned on some music, and began crying. I was ready to die. After sitting there an hour and a half waiting to die, I was still alive. So I took the hose off, threw it away, and went home with a severe headache. Even though I believed God had saved me from my suicide attempt, I continued on with my self-destructive behavior.

Three times I tried to overdose on my pain medication. I would get sick for three days, but I lived on. By this time I had regained about sixty-five percent of the use of my leg and twenty-five percent of the use of my arm. I felt horrible from all the drinking and drugs I was doing at the time, but I was still blaming these problems on the accident. I cursed God and turned from my friends and family. It was the darkest chapter of my life.

CHAPTER IV
My First Job

In 1984 I got a job at Lewis Gale Hospital in Salem, Virginia, as a physical therapist technician. I had to drive about a hundred and twenty miles a day round trip. Since the job involved helping people, I liked what I was doing. One day a girl who worked with me noticed an article in the newspaper about a bicycling event for Multiple Sclerosis (MS). The course was a hundred and fifty miles that had to be covered in two days. The foundation sent me a shirt to wear in getting supporters for my participation. Everyone who donated signed the shirt and enabled me to raise $300 for MS in the two weeks before the event. I had just gotten a new bike and was ready to go. About one hundred fifty people had volunteered to ride.

I thought I would do well but was left behind early on the first day by the other really good riders. Because I was used to leading the field, this was a great challenge for me. We rode ninety-nine miles the first day. With ten miles left to our destination, my legs began to hurt unbearably. I stopped at the next checking station that was four miles from the finish line for that day. I got off my bike, went over to a medical worker, and described my symptoms. She massaged my legs and asked if I had been eating bananas. I replied that I did not like bananas and wondered what that had to do with riding a bike. She said that bananas contain potassium and explained why that was important. She let me feel the knotted-up muscles that were producing the cramps. The knots were as big as golf balls. I finished for that day and ate bananas that night.

The next morning I felt great, but a new problem soon arose. When I had gone to buy new bike shoes before the race, the store I went to had Size 10 only. I wear a Size 13, but I had bought the Size 10 anyway. My feet started hurting almost as soon as I got on my bike. By the time I had ridden forty miles, I had excruciating pain in my right foot. I stopped at a checking station; fortunately, a doctor was there. When I took off my shoe, he saw that the toenail on my big toe was almost off. He quickly removed it and said I could not continue with the race. I begged him to let me go on with the others, but he drove me in his car up to the finish line and let me out. Quitting the race bothered me deeply, but I knew there would be other opportunities in the future. When those times came, I would definitely have the right size shoe!

On the job at Lewis Gale, my supervisor wanted to keep me, but I was drinking, using drugs, and missing work two or three times a week. I finally quit because I liked partying better than I did working.

My next job was working for a road contractor out of Buchanan. I started out as a flagman, the most boring job anyone could have. The two-lane dirt road we were paving was out in the country where cars came by only once every two hours. That summer I got the best tan I have ever had. There was a thicket beside the place where I was working, and in a week's time it would be bulldozed over by the company doing the work. One day I went into the thicket and found a stick with a vine wrapped around it so tightly that the vine had grown into the wood. I didn't know at the time that the plant indented into the sapling was Japanese honeysuckle. I took the stick home and started carving on it. After all the bark was off, the stick was really pretty. I gave the stick to a girl who lived next to the worksite. She liked what I had done and said I should start carving walking sticks. Acting on her advice, I started making canes and walking sticks out of young trees with honeysuckle twisted around them. When I removed the honeysuckle, the groove left reminded me of a candy cane.

It took me about twelve years to get to the point of making the sticks right. I sell sticks now for anywhere between $35 and $150 and go to shows at places like Douthat State Park Arts and Crafts show and the Sugar Maple Festival in Monterey in Highland County. That was where I got into trouble. A friend of mine was selling lamps, and I was selling my sticks out of the back of my truck. A woman approached and informed us that we could not do that without a merchant's license. That was news to both of us.

The highway construction job, which was my main support, continued for about three summers. Then I got a job at the golf course near my house. I would go to work at 5:30 a.m. and get off at 1:30 p.m. Mowing the greens had to be done before the golfers showed up at dawn when they could hardly see the ball. I got to play free, but golf was not my favorite sport since my handicap involving my right arm made swinging the club very difficult. I spent only one summer at this job and moved on the next year to trapping gypsy moths for the Virginia Forestry Service. I would drive to different counties (Alleghany, Craig, Botetourt, and Giles) to trap the moths for a salary-plus-mileage pay. I really liked this job because I was required to hike back into the woods to check the moth traps we had set. I saw a lot of wonderful things that summer: waterfalls, beautiful views, and a cave that went 235 feet into the ground with fog coming out of it. In the course of the summer, I met a female forestry service secretary in Blacksburg who had never gone canoeing. I invited her up to the Jackson River to go canoeing, and she brought me a sweater that had three canoes on it, one of which looked just like the canoe I was using that day. After sixteen years, I still have the shirt, but the job lasted only one summer.

My next summer job was at the Elks Boys' Camp at Nimrod Hall. I was employed to do maintenance and enjoyed this job very much as it involved working with the campers when I got the chance. Once a week I took the campers hiking on Beard's Mountain. My favorite spot was a cliff from which I could look for miles and miles. This work was very challenging as I did a lot of lifting and operated a tractor with a brushhog. Every summer for four years I returned to this job because it gave me a lot of satisfaction. Every day after work, I would go swimming in the Cowpasture River with my goggles and my fins and look in the bottom of the river for rocks I used to make necklaces. Over the years I found some interesting shapes, including a dog and a man's face. One day, late in the afternoon, I spotted a beaver under water and then another one. On other days I would hold worms and feed the fish out of my hand. These were thrilling experiences to get so close to these creatures of nature.

After a year of staying at home making walking sticks and selling them, I applied for a position at Boys' Home, a home for boys ages nine to eighteen with apartments for those who have finished high school. The population is a mixture of boys without parents, those who could not be controlled at home, and those referred by the state department of corrections. I served as the athletic coordinator, charged with the responsibility of getting the residents involved in a variety of activities: basketball, swimming, biking, and lifting weights. As I played alongside the boys, I served as a mentor to listen to their problems.

I also led a scout troop made up of Boys' Home boys. During the first camping trip I took them on, we encountered rain, hail, lightning, and high winds. The hail lasted only a few minutes while we were hiking to the campsite. Once we were on the ridge at the place where we planned to put up our tents, the rain started coming down like pouring out of a bucket. Lightning followed the rain. Imagine being responsible for twenty boys on the highest spot around when lightning was lighting up the sky. Those who got their tents up felt like the wind might rip them and their tents away at any minute. There was one bright spot. When the rain stopped for an hour, one of the leaders started a fire with a fire log he had brought. It burned brightly for an hour, and everyone felt better. Then the wind and the rain returned in all their fury. Everything we had was soaked; it was, to say the least, a sleepless night. When it was light enough to see, the other leader and I decided to break camp. Going down the mountain, we came across an old creek bed that had been completely dry when we had crossed it the night before. Now the water was up to the waists of the boys as I took them across. Because of the storm, the boys did not fulfill enough of the requirements for their badges, so another overnight was in order when the weather would cooperate.

While I was still working part time at Boys' Home, I applied for the position of substitute teacher for the Alleghany Highlands Public Schools and was hired. I was shocked to see how kindergarteners behaved. I felt like the Kindergarten Cop from the movie with Arnold Swartzenegger. By halfway through the day, I had lost my voice and could not talk above a whisper, so I made up a story to get the kids' attention. I pointed to the scar on my head that goes all the way around showing where I was scalped in the wreck and began a tall tale about how my dog and I were walking in the woods when a bear attacked me. "Was it a grizzly?" one little boy asked.

"Why not?" I thought, and agreed that it was and said it had scalped me. The attack had made me angry, so I beat it up and dragged it home and kept it as a pet. The children were good the rest of the day. Maybe I shouldn't have told that tall tale, but it worked.

Once when I was teaching an eleventh grade geometry class, one girl said to me, "I have seen you on TV." I replied that she must have seen the news about my triathlon competition. No one knew what that was, so I explained that those in the race had to compete in three events: kayaking, biking, and running. After they understood what I was saying, the students became very cooperative.

I have never had a job that did not teach me many lessons. Working for Boys' Home and the Alleghany schools has been especially rewarding. When these jobs were winding down, I went looking for another job. My first stop was Cliffview Golf Course on the other side of Covington where I talked to the owner about working there. He said, "Well, Keith, let me think about it." I got the impression that he didn't think I could handle the physical requirements of the work since I had only one good hand. About two weeks later, he called and gave me the job. I was really excited about working outdoors. The job involved weed eating about 75 percent of the time and mowing 25 percent of the time. I would weed eat banks around ponds; actually, sometimes I stood up in a boat to reach the part I could not access from the bank. I guess you could call me a professional weed whacker. Although the job was physically demanding and hot, I felt like the workout I was getting 6-8 hours a day was excellent training for me. The sheer beauty of the surroundings—the cliffs and the mountains—made all my effort worthwhile. Both my bosses were extra nice to me and encouraged me to work harder toward my goals.

While I was working there one day, a fairly easy one, a guy came up to me and apologetically said, "I just hit a flying goose!"

My question was, "Where? With your car?"

"No! With my golf ball! I nailed him, and he is dead on hole number one."

"That is pretty amazing," I said, "to be able to kill a goose with a golf ball."

"Yes, but I missed the hole," he sadly reported.

I didn't believe him, so I went up to number one hole, and, sure enough, there lay the dead goose. So much for routine days at the golf course!

CHAPTER V
Let the Good Times Roll

The first time I met Randy Dolin, I thought we were going four-wheeling in his little Subaru. While he was driving through mud holes and over mounds, I looked beside me and saw a burlap sack lying beside my feet on the floorboard. To my surprise, when I asked him what was in the bag, he replied, "Two rattlesnakes. We are going snake hunting."

"Oh, no!" I thought. "Not another one of those!" He stopped the car, and got out his tongs to try to catch a snake. He was unsuccessful, and I was glad. This was a strange beginning for a continuing friendship.

The summer I was nineteen, I got a new raft. I asked two friends to go along with me to raft the swollen Cowpasture River. Due to heavy rains, the water was about seven feet above flood stage. The three of us had been drinking beer and Wild Turkey and were feeling no pain. We were taking a five mile trip which started out easy. We were laid back, drinking, and telling stories. I warned them to be ready for the falls which was a seven foot drop; they assured me they were quite capable. We hit the first rapids and went about six feet before reaching the falls. We dropped five feet and hit a hydraulic, a force that kept the raft and the rafter down in a hole. The raft folded in half when it hit the hydraulic. Jeff, who was sitting in the front, smacked into me where I was sitting on the back. We were probably in the hole for fifteen seconds. When the raft was thrown clear, we were all still in the raft; so was the beer cooler. We could not believe what had just happened to us. We started shouting for joy and drinking to celebrate our escape.

Another time friends and I were on the Cowpasture, each in separate canoes. The river was up about two-and-a-half feet. We were canoeing from Griffith's Knob to the Green Hole and had to go through the same falls that had given us nightmares when we were rafting earlier. To avoid another mishap, we stopped before we got to the falls and scouted them out. Some of us were shotgunning beer. For those who have never tried this procedure, it involves making a hole in the bottom of the can, pulling the tab, and sucking the contents out in a few seconds. I reminded the first one going over the fall to paddle when he hit the first set of rapids. Instead of paddling, he waved. Of course, his canoe got sucked into the hole, turning over with him under it. It was funny at first until he went over the falls still under the canoe. Then we became horrified, not knowing what to do. The hydraulic at the bottom of the falls spit him out, and he swam over to his overturned canoe and lay on it. We all followed him over the falls to rescue him. His back and legs were a mangled mess, but otherwise he was unhurt. We continued on our way, drinking and having a good time.

One Saturday morning, Edwin and I decided to canoe down the Bullpasture. We got all out gear ready, and I called my cousin Rodney to see if he would like to join us. He was interested and, since he needed another person in his canoe, he would ask a friend to come with him. He assured me he was used to rough water. The river we were going on was about three feet up and had Class 3 to Class 5 rapids. As we started down the river, we came through a gorge with some pretty gnarly rapids. It was exhilarating, to say the least.

We came to a small pool with a waterfall off to one side. The fall was about five feet high, and at the bottom was a huge rock. Water was veering off in two directions, so I waited at the top, and Edwin waited at the bottom while Rodney and his friend went over the falls. They were unable to steer around the rock, so they hit it squarely with the bow of the canoe. They thought they were going to die. Even though the canoe got sucked under the rock and stuck, both boys were able to escape.

We couldn't retrieve the canoe without some equipment we didn't have. I remembered that a friend of mine lived near the place where we were stuck. When we climbed about 150 yards straight up to the top of a massive cliff to start looking for his house, we actually ran right into it. He had a come-along that he allowed us to borrow. As soon as we attached it to the boat and applied pressure, the come-along broke.

Then we had to climb back up to see if he had another one that was stronger. With the larger tool in hand, we climbed back down to try again. This time it worked. The canoe was folded in half when we got it out, so Rodney and his friend had to walk about a half mile down the gorge pulling the canoe beside them in the water. Edwin and I canoed on down about three miles to where Edwin had parked his truck, got in, and rode to a place where we could pick up the rest of the crew along with the damaged canoe. After that episode, none of us ever went down the Bullpasture again.

However, one August night my friend Randy and I went camping on the Bullpasture River in Highland County. We had been drinking most of the night and got up early to go hiking. We went up a winding road on the Shenandoah Mountain and took the first trail we came to. Even in the early morning, the heat was oppressive. About a mile and a half up the mountain, the trail ended, and we stopped to rest. When we got to the top, we watched a storm coming up over Bull Mountain. Randy and I were at such a high elevation that we could see the top and the bottom of the storm much as one would expect to see from an airplane. That was the most beautiful storm I have ever seen as the bolts of lightning flashed from the top to the bottom of the clouds.

I wanted to go back the same way we came, but Randy wanted to try a different trail, so I followed his suggestion. We had one sixteen-ounce bottle of water. That was not enough. We walked down the mountain over many ridges and realized finally that we were lost in a wilderness with no other humans around. The water had given out long before we finally came to a creek; it was the best water I have ever had. One of the rules for finding a way to civilization is to follow a creek downstream, for it will lead to bigger bodies of water. So that is what we did. We came upon a field full of deer that were so tame that we could almost feed them out of our hand. We spent about an hour with them and longed for a camera. Then we walked and walked, trying to get back to my truck. Eight-and-a half hours later, we came out of the woods onto a paved road. We walked three miles before we came to a house where a man was washing a car. When we asked for a drink of water, he complied. Then I asked him how to get back to my truck. He wanted to know where it was parked. When I explained where we had started our adventure, he was able to point us in the right direction. The bad news was that it was still seventeen miles to where we needed to be. He said, "How would you like some pot pies? My wife just made them."

I said, "Sure!" because I hadn't eaten for twenty-four hours.

Randy looked at me with a question in his eyes. "Home-made pot pies?" he murmured.

These were not little pot pies, I can tell you, and each of us ate two. With full bellies and grateful hearts, we thanked these good people. Our new friend then gave us a ride to my truck. We said that we wished we could pay him, but we had no money. His reply was that the important thing was that we were safe. Later on I picked two gallons of blackberries and delivered them to his house. He was very grateful.

Sometimes I wonder how I survived long enough to write this book. When Michael Jordan was famous, another Michael Jordan who was my friend could have told this part of the story. The Michael I knew, Randy, and I decided about ten o'clock one night to go camping. It was five degrees below zero at home and ten degrees below zero at Pete's Cave on North Mountain where we planned to spend the rest of the night. Randy was supposed to meet us there at midnight; it was a four mile hike from the road. Michael and I got there a half hour before the agreed-on time. We set up camp in one of the twenty crevices surrounding the cave and tried to get a fire started, but our hands were too cold to hold the matches. We kept trying down to our last match. Randy finally arrived, warm from the walk, and succeeded in starting a fire. We explored the cave which was the usual fifty degrees and really wanted to stay inside, but we made ourselves go back to the campsite for reasons that were clear to me then but escape me now. With a tarp over the crevice to keep out the wind and its spooky sounds, we made camp, got as comfortable as possible, and went to sleep.

The roaring fire we had built lured Michael ever closer to its warmth. In the middle of the night, Randy got up and found that the fire had burned the down in Michael's sleeping bag, and his boots' rubber soles were smoldering. Randy took a bottle of pop and poured it over the boots to put out the fire. He tried to wake Michael, but he slept on. The next day, we got up and got ready to leave. Michael walked off the mountain with his sock showing out the bottom of his burned boot. He was in front as we went down the mountain. We smelled the worst odor we had ever encountered and finally figured out it was the burned down in the sleeping bag Michael had stuffed into his backpack. The rest of the way down the mountain, we put Michael about a hundred yards behind us with the wind blowing his way. We threw his sleeping bag in the back of the truck and headed for home. At that time we felt he had very little in common with the famous man with the same name.

Canoeing always leaves me with a hearty appetite. One day I had just come from the river and had gone home starved. Mom had gotten some beef jerky which I thought was for the family to eat, so my sister Heather and I ate about ten pieces. When Mom got home, I told her the beef jerky was great and suggested she buy some more of the same brand. She asked me where I got it, and I told her I had found it in the cabinet. She gave me a surprised look and said in a disbelieving tone, "The beef jerky you just ate, Keith, was dog food." That was the last time I ate jerky without reading the label.

Another time, a group of us decided to raft the New River on the first day of April. We had gone over the night before the scheduled rafting, and about ten of us went down to the river after dark to look at the water level. It was up sufficiently to assure us of an exciting ride. On the way back to the tent, my friends wanted to stop at the New River Bridge that crosses the gorge at 876 feet above the river. About seven of the group climbed up the abutments to the deck of the bridge. The abutments had holes in them which allowed the climbers to look down to the water. By the time they got to the top, one of them exclaimed, "Boy, that is a long way down!" This venture was typical of the daredevil stunts my friends and I used to pull.

The next day was perfect for being on the water, even though it was supposed to have been cold. By that time the river was twelve feet up and roaring through the gorge. I rode in the front of the boat, and my wet suit was soaked. We closed out the day with a pig roast and eleven kegs of beer for the two hundred or so people that were camped there. There were bands and dances, and everyone was happy until the next day when most of them were sick. I enjoyed the adventure so much that I went back four more times in the summers following.

A friend of mine and I went to Canada several years ago on a fishing, hiking trip. We stopped at Niagara Falls by way of a gambling casino on the Canadian side of the falls. Since we were in the casino, I played three games, won all three, and quit while I was ahead. We drove from there north to the French River. It looked more like what we would call a lake. There was so much water there that it was mind-boggling. I set up a tent, ate supper, and went to bed. I was in a deep sleep when I heard the walking stick that I had leaned against the table flop over against the side of the tent. Then I heard something scratching against the coolers outside the tent. I did not know what to do because I was pretty sure my night visitor was a bear. I have never been as scared in my whole life as I was at that moment. After thinking a minute, I opened the flap of my tent and saw the back end of the bear. An experienced fisherman had told me to yell three times if I saw a bear, so that is what I did. The bear left. The rest of the night I lay with a fillet knife beside me and prayed, for I had ten days of wilderness experience still ahead of me!

My friend missed all this because he was staying in a camper. The next day, with no sleep, I drove to Algonquin Park which is the most northerly park in Canada, measuring about half the size of Virginia. On an old dirt road, I came to a sign that said it was 56 kilometers to the park. At the entrance to the park, I purchased a paper with an article about two people who had been killed by a bear in this very park. My friend and I pitched camp about two miles from a supply station where a man would freeze fish that were caught on Cedar Lake and mail them to the home of the one who caught them. I talked to him about the bear problem. He said to urinate in a circle around the tent and build a big fire to keep the bears away. The man scent repelled the animals, and we didn't have any more trouble. With wolves howling in the background, I went to sleep hoping the solution for keeping bears away would work for wolves too. That trip cured me of all fears. I enjoyed it fully.

CHAPTER VI
Favorite Pastimes

As my grandfather had predicted when I was two, hiking became my first love. I have tackled every mountain in Alleghany County as well as those in other places in Virginia, North Carolina, West Virginia, Colorado, and Canada. Every year on my birthday I go to Griffith's Knob near Clifton Forge, a part of Rough Mountain. It is one of the hardest hikes in this part of the country. It looks like a dry, desolate place, but when I walk up it—and that is straight up—I see six waterfalls in a gorge that is not visible from the road. The headwaters are formed from a pool that is so beautiful it looks like something from a nature calendar. After a two-hour climb, I have to scale a fifty-foot cliff to get to the top. Standing on the peak, I can see 360 degrees around me. It is a God-given treasure.

One year I picked Morrell mushrooms as I walked up the knob with Abby, my dog. After I picked the mushrooms, I decided to go down into the gorge to take some pictures.

As I walked on a narrow passageway, I got my camera set up, ready to take a picture. It was the middle of April, and I was focusing on Abby, prepared to take a shot, when I saw something move in the corner of the picture. It was a copperhead curled up in a lethargic condition because the weather was still cold. I put the camera away and got the dog to follow me farther down the gorge. When I had gone about twenty-five feet, I came upon another copperhead about two feet away from me. I had actually walked by it coming up the gorge. Surely I would see no more copperheads that day! Fifty feet farther on the rim of the gorge, I saw another one. I walked down to the creek and carved into the bark of a tree, "Copperhead Hollow." The tree with its inscription still stands today. I continue to go back even though I know the snakes are there.

Since fishing is a close second among my passions, a hunting and fishing trip to Colorado was a true highlight of my life. My dad, two friends of the family, and I went to a place called Pitkin about forty miles from Gunnison. It has been called the prettiest place in the state, and I accept that evaluation. We arrived at nightfall, got everything unpacked, and went to sleep in a cottage we had rented for two weeks. The other three were hunters, and I was a fisherman. The next morning I went for a mile walk and stopped to talk to a man who ran a little shop nearby. He told me that I should never have gone walking until I had about three days to adjust to the thin atmosphere. The elevation at our quarters was 9,610 feet above sea level. He was right about not exerting right away. I became nauseated, my nose bled, and I was sick for about two days.

I could not believe the fishing on Gold's Creek! I caught 100 native trout in two hours. I could look down in the fishing hole and pick out which trout I wanted to catch. My friends and I ate all the fish I was allowed to keep–six every day. We baked some and fried others. It was the greatest fishing I have ever done in such a short period of time.

One day, after I was acclimated to the oxygen level, I decided to walk up the mountain. The exertion that day didn't bother me like it had the first day. I got near the top of the mountain and thought I was in heaven because it was so beautiful. The peak I was on was surrounded by three lakes. I had to pinch myself to determine that I was still on earth, for I have never been anywhere else so breathtaking. I thanked God for creating that wonderful masterpiece.

About a week into our trip, one of our party killed a 700 pound female elk about three miles from our camp. He came to ask me to help him carry the meat back to camp. He cut the meat and bagged it, and I carried it back in a huge backpack. It took three round trips that day, a total of eighteen miles up and down the slope. I figured I carried about eighty-five pounds each time. Because the weather was cold enough to preserve the meat, we waited until the next day to get the rest. When we got back to the carcass the next morning, a mother bear and two cubs were eating the innards he had put a hundred yards up the slope. We cut the meat off in a hurry, came off the mountain, and never went back.

About the last day we were there, I went walking in the woods and met a man who said there was silver in the area. I found enough slabs to bring one back to each of my nieces and nephews. At the fishing hole, a prospector told me there was gold in Gold's Creek. I think sometimes about going back to Pitkin to pan for gold, but the winters are so cold. Someday, when I get enough money to finance another trip, I may go back during a milder season. In the meantime, I will treasure the memories of my Colorado adventure.

One September morning, my dad, my friend Keith Atkins, and I set out for Hatteras, North Carolina, on the Atlantic Ocean below Nag's Head. When we got to Norfolk, we heard about a hurricane headed for Nag's Head, but we were sure it would miss us. However, when we stopped at a little grocery store near the lighthouse on Cape Hatteras, the wind began to blow, making a loud, eerie sound as it tossed the light wires around in the air. The rain was coming down in sheets as the trees bent almost to the ground. We went on to the motel and arrived there just at nightfall. About eleven o'clock that night, I went out into the parking lot. The water from the ocean had come through the holes the wind had blown in the dunes and was up to my knees. I called friends of mine at home and told them I thought I was going to die. I didn't see any way we could survive that storm, but I prayed harder than I had ever prayed before.

After the storm passed, we could not leave for two days, for the sand dunes in Nag's Head were blown across the road, making it impassable, so we went fishing because that was what we had come to do. I caught so many fish that day that I had blisters on my hands from pulling them in. I caught red drums, flounder, whiting, skates, spots, croakers—you name it, I caught it, and my friends and I had a massive fish fry. Something about this experience reminds me of the story of Jesus and the storm on the Sea of Galilee that was followed by his disciples catching fish.

CHAPTER VII
A Close-knit Family

When I was young, I used to stay with my grand-mother five days a week. She was married to a man people called Popeye because of his massive upper arms. Officially, they were Todd and Mary Lucy Nicely. MawMaw had a cow called Star. Every morning she would get up at daylight and milk the cow. Then she would bring in the milk and churn the cream that was ready and make butter and buttermilk. I can see her now pressing the butter into the wooden mold and pouring the buttermilk into a crock for the family to drink and for her to use in cooking. She was a wonderful cook. One thing I remember, besides my uncle crumbling cornbread into a glass of buttermilk, is the custard she made. She sold the milk that the family could not use. She had the reputation of making the best butter and buttermilk in the county. In addition to all this work, she kept children for working parents. She would keep up to twenty-two children a day. Over the years she documented taking care of at least five hundred children. Unbelievable!

My aunt had a station wagon at the time. She would come on Thursdays to help my grandmother because that was the day the Jane Colby plant, a clothing factory in town, would take all its discarded material to the dump in nearby Millboro. The two women watched until the truck passed the house and then piled all of us in the car to drive up to the dumpster to retrieve huge rolls of material which they planned to use in making quilts and aprons. We kids were so bored with nothing to do but watch them become excited over their finds for the day. We were glad when the wagon was so full it would not hold anything else but us. Then we knew we were through until the next Thursday.

My grandmother lived on a dirt road with very little traffic. A hill rose behind her house and then gradually sloped until it came to a drop-off leading to a swamp and the river. As you can imagine, we children were not allowed to go there, but we were very curious—so curious, in fact, that one day my cousin Rodney, who at eleven was a year older than I, sneaked off with me and went over the hill to explore. We found an old house that was falling in. We took some boards off the roof and pulled out some papers and read them. They were letters written by a man in service during World War II to his sweetheart. It got to be two o'clock, and we knew we had better get back where we belonged. On our way back, we stumbled across some coiled copper pipe and a couple of old gallon jugs filled with some kind of clear liquid. We couldn't get the top off, so we took one of our treasures back to the house. That jug was so heavy that we had to take turns carrying it up the hill.

Grandmother was outside and saw us coming. All hope of getting by with our disobedience was gone. "What do you have in that jar?" she demanded. The top that we had struggled with, she quickly removed. At five-foot-two, she was skinny as a rail but strong as an ox. She took a big whiff as the top came off, and announced that what we had carried home was white lightning, a moonshiner's delight. She made Rodney and me pour it out and told us never to go back down the hill and never to pick up any more bottles. We were excited about our find and went back many times to see what else we could find. Poor Grandmother!

Our whole community used to get together every fall at Grandmother's house and make apple butter in a big copper kettle. We would all stand around and talk while the adults drank coffee and took turns stirring the apple butter. Later in the fall, when the weather turned cold, we would gather to slaughter hogs. Again there was a boiling pot; this time it was scalding water for getting the bristles off the hog's skin. Half the hog would be immersed in the hot water at a time. If the water was just right, the bristles could be scraped off easily. If it was too hot, the hair would be singed and be a job to remove.

When I was about twelve, the man I looked up to the most in this world, my grandfather, died from lung cancer. I watched him turn yellow and struggle with pain for a year. I was relieved when he died. He had one of the biggest funerals I ever remember. Even though I was just twelve, I learned a lot about cancer and the heartache it can cause. I will see him again. I did not know this when I lost him, but I know it now.

Getting back to my immediate family, I need to tell you about my sisters, Mary Paige and Heather. Paige is a year younger than I, and Heather is four years younger than she. Paige has always liked trying new things. She read in a book once that lying out in the snow on a sunny day would produce a spectacular tan. After it snowed one day and the sun came out, she went outside in a bikini to sunbathe. She didn't get a tan, but she did get as cold as an icicle. One other time Paige and I were eating on the porch. I took a chicken leg that Paige really wanted and ran into the house, slamming the door behind me. Paige came in hot pursuit and ran into the glass of the storm door. The glass shattered and cut her forearm badly. That night I got whipped with a belt for causing Paige to get hurt.

Paige has done well in her adult life. With her husband she operates a physical therapy business. During her training for certification, she had as one project tying her shoe with one hand. She had watched me struggle with this in the early days of my disability and thought it would be easy. After working with this problem for a long time, she began to see a little of what I had been going through trying to accomplish old tasks with the loss of one limb. She never did learn how to tie that shoe!

She and her husband produced two sons, Andrew and Adam. Andrew, the older of her boys, was in a duathlon in Roanoke when he was thirteen years old. In spite of my argument that he should ride a full-sized bike, he chose a twenty-inch stunt bike to ride ten miles up and down ridges. Then he ran four miles with me. Andrew did well with the bike he was riding, but I felt he could have done better with a larger bike. Nevertheless, we each came in third in our separate divisions, and I was proud of him.

Heather was a different breed. The baby of the family, she was the shy and timid one, the almost perfect sister. She could get along with anybody, and she and I have always been very close. Now a single mom with three beautiful girls, she is the superintendent of her Sunday school and takes good care of the kids.

One spring day after I quit drinking, Heather let me take Kelcy, her oldest daughter, walking. We went to the Devil's Marble Yard near Glasgow. There is an old Indian tale about this area. Two missionaries stayed two years with the Indians until a drought came. The Indians blamed the white men for the absence of rain and burned them at the stake. When the missionaries died, the rocks on the nearby cliff came tumbling down, forming an unusual display of marble as a fitting monument. It is truly a beautiful sight to see. Kelcy, just six at the time, was tripping over everything, and her legs were full of scratches. I said, "Kelcy, can't you see where you are going?"

"Not that well," she said.

I continued to walk, holding her hand to keep her from falling. We got to our destination, the Devil's Marble Yard, and the view was spectacular. Imagine an area with marble a half mile wide and a mile high at the highest peaks. Benches were created by the falling rocks that appeared to fall down the mountain just as the legend said, making this almost indescribable mass. We walked back to the truck, stopped to buy some ice cream, and I took Kelcy home. After I told Heather about Kelcy's eyesight problem, she took her daughter to an eye specialist, and he fitted her for glasses. She sees well now. I enjoyed the adventure with my young niece immensely, and we still talk about our day together. Someday I will take her and her sisters back.

Mom and Dad are two people I love very much. Dad taught me how to play basketball and football and how to fish and hunt. He even taught me how to defend myself. My accident was about as hard on my dad as it was on me, and, in some strange way, it created a barrier between us. He had lost the son he had always wanted, the gifted athlete, and he had instead a crippled teenager who had a multitude of problems. Although that barrier continues to separate us today, he is fiercely protective of me

Once, a year after the accident, we went on a four-day fishing trip to Nag's Head. At the time I had only 5 percent use of my arm and 30 percent use of my leg; I walked with a brace. In the course of the fishing, I was walking toward my dad and accidentally tripped over a man's shark pole. This huge man became very verbally angry and would not stop yelling long enough to accept my apology. Dad heard the commotion and told the man either to get his stuff together and leave or get thrown off the pier. The man got his equipment packed in less than a minute and was gone. No matter where I was or what I was doing, my dad was always there but not always in an understanding frame of mind.

Another time Dad wanted me to rake the yard. I had about 20 percent use of my arm at that time, so I told him it was too hard to rake with one hand. After going out to the garage and thinking about the problem, I got a piece of PVC pipe six inches in diameter and twenty-eight inches long. I looked long and hard at it and decided what to do. Finally, after cutting, heating, and drilling the pipe, I inserted a wooden handle that I could grasp and screws that would hold a rake in place. With this device I could rake the yard with my one good arm. All the next day, I used my new invention to clear the yard of leaves as my dad had asked. I wanted with all my heart to please him.

After I saw how well my new tool worked, I called Virginia Prosthetics and went over to Roanoke to the office and showed the people there what I had. One man I talked to makes prosthetic devices himself and strongly suggested that I should get a patent. I followed his suggestion and got a provisional patent that lasted two years, a very inexpensive process. Then I went to Norfolk and got a prosthetics company to make a commercial model. Right after that, I was invited to a show featuring devices for people with handicaps. My device was considered the newest and one of the best in the show. Someone from a Roanoke television station came and asked me to step outside for an interview. I was sweating bullets. A reporter from the <u>Roanoke Times</u> asked me questions also and published a feature article in his paper. After I used my invention to accommodate a golf club, I was on two of the Roanoke stations again.

Actually, I have found many uses for this device for a person with the use of one arm in addition to raking and golfing: sweeping, mopping, and hoeing—to name a few— but the possibilities are unlimited. I have been to shows from Washington, D.C. to Roanoke, and many predicted I would be a rich man. However, to realize any money from my invention, I would have to produce and market it, and the risk involved in putting a lot of money into this venture seemed too great for me to consider just then. At present I have a patent on my forearm assistive device and someday will see my way clear to produce and sell it because I feel it has the potential for helping a lot of people. What I need is a sponsor who can supply the financial backing I need to bring this dream to a reality.

When I was twelve years old, my family went with another family to Myrtle Beach. Their children were about the same age as my next youngest sister and I. One morning Dad and I and the other father and son were going out on a commercial boat in Murrell's Inlet to fish in the ocean. Before we left at 7:00 a.m., we had a big breakfast. I had four eggs, two pieces of sausage, two pieces of toast, and juice We boarded the boat and had gone about two miles out into the inlet before we hit the ocean. The other boy and I were riding on the deck of the boat, convinced that this was the trip of a lifetime.

After we left the protection of the inlet and entered the ocean, it was very choppy with high winds. Almost at once I got seasick and began to feed my wonderful breakfast to the fish as I leaned over the rail. I vomited about eight times, got clammy, and turned green. As a matter of fact, everybody on the boat except the crew and one passenger joined me at the rail. I realized I shouldn't have eaten such a big breakfast and will remember not to repeat this incident if I go deep-sea fishing again. We were too sick to think about fishing, and Dad even offered the captain $200 if he would take me and him back to shore. The captain refused, so we just toughed it out. In all my accidents, I never had such pain and agony as I felt that day. Death would have been a welcome relief. We were sick the whole day until we reentered the inlet on the way back in. When we got off the boat, I kissed the ground we walked on.

A story I grew up with was about one summer day before I was born, when Mom and Dad were traveling to Highland County, the least populated county this side of the Mississippi River. Their destination was the Bulllpasture River where they planned to trout fish. Dad pulled up in front of a home where a black man was sitting on the porch in a rocking chair. Mom got out of the car, walked up to the porch, and asked for directions, but the man would not answer. Dad was aware, as Mom was not, that the figure sitting in the chair was carved from wood. Needless to say, Dad was laughing his head off as Mom tried repeatedly to communicate. It was not until she got back to the truck that she realized she had been set up.

When I told my cousin this story recently, he topped it, for he owned the farm where this took place. It seems that, on another occasion, an FBI agent was traveling from McDowell in Highland County to Millboro in Bath County. He stopped along the way to ask directions at my cousin's house where my dad had tricked my mom. The black man did not answer FBI questioning either. Just then, a breeze made the figure rock back and forth. The agent pulled his gun on the dummy as the man of the house opened the door and informed the visitor that the man in the chair was wooden. A very embarrassed FBI agent quickly left the premises. At some point, the Smithsonian Institute offered $6,000 for the carving, but the owners refused to sell. Two years later the man was stolen from the porch. If you visit the Smithsonian and see my friend's artwork, you will know how it ended up there.

I have another family member with an interesting story to tell, my Uncle Michael. It was 1993 on a clear June day. Everything was quiet that afternoon in Niceleytown with not a cloud in the sky. Michael arrived home from work and took note of the horse in the pasture trying to eat the grass that was "greener on the other side of the fence" and his dog that was tied to the same fence. He decided to clear his gutter and braced his ladder up against the fence close to the animals. Out of nowhere came a spectacular bolt of lightning followed by a tremendous boom. The lightning hit a tree to which the fence was tacked. The horse and dog were killed instantly as the lightning ran down the fence. The bolt ran down the fence, melting the fence as it went, and struck the ladder where Michael stood. The electricity ran into Michael's boots and up his body, coming out at his elbow. Meanwhile, it also brushed his son Josh who was coming out of the garage. He was not injured, but he was very scared for his dad.

Michael was knocked to the ground where he lay unable to speak coherently. His wife called my house, and I went immediately to offer help. I felt he needed to see a doctor, so she rushed him to the hospital where the examining doctor assured her that there were no serious injuries. He sent Michael home without treatment. The speech problem cleared up the next day, but he is still scared of lightning. To this day nobody still has any idea why the lightning struck the way it did.

CHAPTER VIII
My Nine Lives

Earlier I recounted the details of my first wreck, but I didn't tell you there were eight more to follow. Three stood out in my mind as worse than the others. One night I was out partying at a friend's house. I was about as high as a Georgia pine, and my friend said there was a big ditch nearby that I couldn't get my truck through. I accepted the challenge, and he and I got into my truck and tried to get across the ditch. We didn't make it. Our heads cracked the windshield as we hit the ditch going about forty miles an hour, and the truck was totaled. We struggled back up to his house and slept off the effects of the alcohol. When I woke up, I was in great pain, but I had learned exactly nothing from this experience.

Another time, when I was twenty-one, some friends and I were partying at Walton's Dairy on the Cowpasture River. All of us were drinking heavily and having a good time. I met two girls and asked them if they wanted to go four-wheeling in my Blazer. They readily agreed, so I asked a cousin of mine to go along. First, we went over some back roads on the dairy property and then turned toward an old ford in the river which I did not know had been washed out in the flood of 1985. We were going pretty fast when we suddenly felt nothing under us. The truck was tilted with the rear end straight up and the nose in the river. I asked all the passengers if they were okay, and they answered that they were. We got out of the truck and spent the night with the Waltons who gave my cousin and me a ride home the next morning.

When I got home, I called a wrecker from Clifton Forge, and a friend took me in his truck as the wrecker followed us back to my stranded vehicle. The driver of the wrecker hooked up with the truck and began pulling. The front wheels of the wrecker came up off the ground about six feet, but my truck was not moving. My friend, at the request of the wrecker operator, hooked the back of his truck up to the front of the wrecker in order to keep the wrecker wheels down. It worked! They were able with the wrecker and the truck to easily pull my vehicle out of the water. The wrecker operator charged me only twenty dollars since he had to have help. Fortunately, my friend did not ask that I pay him the difference.

About two years later, I was camping with friends at the Bullpasture River. There was a little side road nearby that a friend and I took. The road was very rough and accessible only to four-wheel-drive vehicles such as the Blazer I was driving. I told my friend to put a seat belt on, but he didn't feel it was necessary until we went over the first bump. We stayed up in the air longer than we were on the ground. He told me at the end of the ride that he would never get in a vehicle with me again, but I had kept him safe.

About 10:30 the next morning I left for the forty-five minute drive home. I rounded a curve going up a hill and was so drunk that I must have passed out. Right in the worst part of the curve, the shoulder of the road fell away to a sheer cliff with a forty-foot drop into a garden with two huge trees growing next to the bank. I veered off the road and hit both trees, clipping them off at the level where I hit them, somersaulted the truck over and over sideways completely in midair, landed on my tires, bounced once, and stopped. For a second, I thought I was flying. The two trees I hit undoubtedly saved my life by breaking the speed of the fall.

I was unhurt, so I got out of the truck and thanked the Lord right before I yelled, "Shit!" when I saw what I had done. I went to the house of a woman who lived about twenty-five yards down the road, and she asked me what had happened. In her opinion, I should have been dead after the distance I had been airborne from the road. I knew then that God had something he wanted me to do and had saved my life for that reason. She gave me seven cups of coffee and was really nice to me. When the state policeman arrived, he could not believe what had happened and was ready to call an ambulance before I assured him that I needed my mother instead. Again, my truck was totaled, but my behavior did not change.

When I was twenty-six years old, I got a Jeep CJ7 with a bored-out 360 engine. It was very powerful; with someone in the back, I could bring the front wheels off the ground. A bunch of my friends and I were four-wheeling one night with about eight trucks and my jeep. I was drinking and smoking dope and was feeling too good. The forestry roads where we were driving had huge dirt mounds at least six feet high to keep unauthorized people like us out. The trucks would get on the mounds and rock until they went over. I had a better way: I simply backed off and gathered enough speed to jump the mounds. I was wearing a seat belt to keep me in the Jeep.

After a while we stopped and drank a few beers before getting back into our vehicles. That time I forgot to fasten my seatbelt, but the boy with me fastened his. We came quickly upon the first mound. We went over, but when the Jeep hit the ground and bounced, it threw me out. The Jeep continued up a steep bank beside the road and rolled over. When this happened, it turned over on me, and the rollbar broke my back in two places before the Jeep rolled on down the hollow with my friend still in it, completely unhurt. That is why people in cars should always wear seatbelts.

The other trucks caught up with us, and my friends put me flat on my back on a mattress in the bed of a truck and took me to the hospital. The doctor in the emergency room checked me briefly and sent me by ambulance to Charlottesville, an hour and a half away. I had cuts on my legs, and the lower vertebrae in my back were broken in two places.

I spent a week in the hospital and three weeks on bed rest at home. After that, I started walking a mile each day with two bricks in my backpack and gradually worked up to five miles with five bricks in my backpack. Then I started backpacking again, wandering around in the woods. This was a type of therapy that worked wonders. My back still bothers me occasionally in the spot where it was broken, but it is a level of pain I can live with.

All this time, God was working in my life. When I was twenty-two, I was living in an apartment in Clifton Forge. I had invited a girl to come over and went to pick her up in my old Jeep Wagoneer that had a 460 engine. How I loved that SUV! We got back to the apartment and began partying, of course, and both had too many beers. Around midnight we left to take her home. We took the back way around town and were coming down a steep hill on a winding road. As I went around a really sharp, left-handed curve, all of a sudden, the passenger door flew open, and my date was flung out. In my drunken stupor and amazement, I stopped the truck and backed up to see if she was okay. She had rolled to the bottom of the ridge we were on. I went down to help her; because of her inebriated state, she had taken the fall well. She assured me she was fine, just shaken up a bit, so I helped her back up the ridge and took her home. Then I went home to bed and slept off the events of the evening.

The next day when my mom was at work, she was told by a coworker that the girl had fallen out of my SUV and was not sure whether or not she was hurt. That night Mom went to prayer meeting. The girl's name was brought up for special prayer. You can imagine what went through my mom's mind! She was scared of what else might be said, but her legs were so shaky that she was not sure she could walk out. The man continued with his story telling that the girl had fallen out of a Jeep and had gone to the hospital to be checked out. The doctor who examined her found a tumor on her hip that she was unaware was there. "God works in mysterious ways," he concluded. I was thankful that, once again, God had let me off the hook. A surgeon removed the tumor, and the girl is fine today. Even with all this, I still was not ready to listen

Contrary to reasonable thinking, this was not the end of my wild adventures. When I was thirty years old, my friend Sandy and her son were with me in a car on a gravel road on North Mountain approaching the top. We parked there and drank a few beers. When we started back down the mountain, we lost our brakes. At a fork in the road, the right hand turn led to Longdale near where I live, and the left hand turn led to Collierstown. Sandy was driving. She chose the left hand road that very quickly took us to a place where a U-turn had a seventy-five foot drop off the side. I grabbed the wheel and turned the car onto a bank that threw it up on a steeper embankment where it turned over. I thought we were doomed until we turned over. We got out of the car and checked her son who was in a car seat.

When we found out he was uninjured, we walked five miles off the mountain. I had a shaggy beard with gray jetting out of it, a pot belly from consuming too many beers, and sunken eyes that were black-rimmed. My life was a total wreck with nowhere to go. I was at the lowest point of my life, but this walk changed all that. We were about halfway to civilization down the other fork when someone spoke to me–God, the Holy Spirit, or an angel. He said, "You have to live your life right and read my Word." I got chills all over my body. From that day on, I put alcohol and other drugs down and started to live my life right with changes for the better. When we finally came to a house, we called the police department. The policeman came up and drove me to the top of the mountain. When he saw where the car was, he said he couldn't get anyone up there to tow it until the next day. We finally got my car back, but I never saw Sandy again. This was my last wreck, for I finally put my faith in God, the Father; God, the Son; and God, the Holy Spirit.

CHAPTER IX
My Road to Salvation

In that summer of 1999, after I wrecked the last time, the Lord truly came into my life, and I was able to quit partying and leave heavy drugs and alcohol alone. I read and reread this passage of scripture from Isaiah 53 until it controlled my life. This Old Testament passage foretold the coming of the Messiah and his suffering and death to purchase our salvation:

53:1 Who hath believed our report? and to whom is the arm of the LORD revealed?

53:2 For he shall grow up before him as a tender plant, and as a root out of a dry ground: he hath no form nor comeliness; and when we shall see him, [there is] no beauty that we should desire him.

53:3 He is despised and rejected of men; a man of sorrows, and acquainted with grief: and we hid as it were

[our] faces from him; he was despised, and we esteemed him not.

53:4 Surely he hath borne our griefs, and carried our sorrows: yet we did esteem him stricken, smitten of God, and afflicted.

53:5 But he [was] wounded for our transgressions, [he was] bruised for our iniquities: the chastisement of our peace [was] upon him; and with his stripes we are healed.

53:6 All we like sheep have gone astray; we have turned every one to his own way; and the LORD hath laid on him the iniquity of us all.

53:7 He was oppressed, and he was afflicted, yet he opened not his mouth: he is brought as a lamb to the slaughter, and as a sheep before her shearers is dumb, so he openeth not his mouth.

53:8 He was taken from prison and from judgment: and who shall declare his generation? for he was cut off out of the land of the living: for the transgression of my people was he stricken.

53:9 And he made his grave with the wicked, and with the rich in his death; because he had done no violence, neither [was any] deceit in his mouth.

53:10 Yet it pleased the LORD to bruise him; he hath put [him] to grief: when thou shalt make his soul an offering for sin, he shall see [his] seed, he shall prolong [his] days, and the pleasure of the LORD shall prosper in his hand.

53:11 He shall see of the travail of his soul, [and] shall be satisfied: by his knowledge shall my righteous servant justify many; for he shall bear their iniquities.

53:12 Therefore will I divide him [a portion] with the great, and he shall divide the spoil with the strong; because he hath poured out his soul unto death: and he was numbered with the transgressors; and he bare the sin of many, and made intercession for the transgressors.

I worked for Camp Accovac that summer, a camp run by the Advent Christian Church. It was one of the hardest jobs I ever had. Once I was burning a bunch of brush when a game warden drove up in his car. The time was 3:40 p.m. The brush fire law in effect prohibits burning before 4:00 p.m., so when I saw him coming, I set my watch forward twenty minutes. His first words were, "Son, do you know what time it is?"

I said, "Yes, sir. It's 4:05!"

"Let me see your watch," he demanded. After looking at it, he commented that it was twenty minutes fast. "I'll let you get by this time," he said, "but it had better not happen again!"

Another incident I remember from that summer happened while I was mowing on a tractor. I felt something was weird about the weather. I looked up in the sky, and it was green. Camp was going on, so I rushed up to where the campers were and told the director to get the children into the basement at once. Hail fell as big as golf balls, and then the wind started blowing. It blew down trees and broke windows, but everyone was safe, and that was my main concern.

A woman cleaned my house at the camp every week while I was there. Since I was working ten to twelve hours a day, my living quarters were always pretty messy. She told me I was the most untidy and disorganized person she knew. I couldn't argue with her then, but I am much better now.

That year was the camp's fiftieth anniversary. There was a group of people at the celebration whom I hadn't seen in years. They had known me during my rebellious years and noticed the extreme change in my life. I told them about how God had spoken to me and had helped me refocus my life. The camp was on a grassy hill with a baseball field at the foot. I mowed, "Happy Fiftieth" in the eighteen inch grass. My artwork was well received by all who observed. I enjoyed the summer of hard work that gave me time by myself to think about God and how he wanted me to live.

About two years after I had quit drinking, my church asked me to teach a Sunday school class of eighteen to twenty-five year old men and women. We met in the dining room, so I fixed breakfast for them many Sundays. Over the course of the year we had venison, different kinds of fish including muskie, and biscuits. The attendance was always good.

Before long I was asked to teach a younger class of teenagers. We did a lot of activities outside of church. One trip I will always remember was canoeing down the Cowpasture River for two days and one night. We started out with about ten people who fished, talked, and swam as we went down the river. Suddenly, a boy in the front of my canoe shouted, "Look at that dog crossing the river!"

"That is no dog!" I informed him. "That is a bear!"

The bear came about halfway across the river before he became aware of the canoes in the river. Then he quickly returned to his original site up in the woods. After we had gone a hundred yards down the river, what appeared to be the same bear crossed the river in front of us. One of the boys docked his canoe and gave chase to the 250 pound wild animal. Fortunately, he never got close because the bear was off and gone. Then we set up camp about a half mile from a bluff that would give us a good view of the surrounding area. On our hike up to the bluff, I discovered a popped helium balloon with a scripture verse attached. I put the verse in my pocket and carried it up to the top where I had devotions. I read the scripture to the group and it went along with every-thing we had been doing all week. Even though I cannot remember now what it said, I thanked God for allowing me to find it and share it with my group. It had a great impact on all of us.

When we got back to camp, some of the boys who had caught fish along the way wanted to know how to cook them. I had brought a Sterno with whale blubber that produced heat. I also had a sterno grill and some seasonings. I taught the boys how to put the herbs on the fish and wrap them in aluminum foil before putting them on the grill. When the food was ready, they thought it was the best fish they had ever eaten, and I was their ideal chef. The next day we went on down the river, stopping at Peters' Bridge. The bridge was about forty-five feet high, but the river was deep, so a few of the most daring jumped in. Then we canoed another mile down the river and got out of the boats to return them to the trucks. The other adult who was with me said it was the most awesome trip of her life. I felt great and shall remember it always as one of my most rewarding adventures.

CHAPTER X
Triathlons

No account of my life would be complete without writing more in detail about my triathlon events. When I was sixteen years old, I had met a boy named Glennie Clark. Some years later we worked together on a construction job. In the winter of 1998, Dr. McCoig asked his receptionist Susan, who was Glennie's wife, if she knew anyone who would like to compete in the canoeing event in a triathlon. She mentioned it to Glennie, and he called me to see if I was interested. Being handicapped the way I am, I thought he was joking, but he assured me he thought I could do the canoeing. I was overjoyed. This would be my first triathlon team event.

There were four members on our team in this Great Greenbrier River Race. Two of us were to canoe four miles, tag a biker who would ride eight miles before tagging a runner who would finish the race. Glennie and I practiced and practiced and practiced in our canoe until we felt we could do the distance required. This was the first triathlon for both of us, and we were extremely excited and nervous.

The race started with our event, and we were paddling well. About halfway through, however, my weak hand began slipping off the oar. I was getting more and more frustrated with myself and asked God to keep my hand in place. As I finished my prayer, I heard Dr. McCoig from the bank cheering us to keep on. At that moment I could clearly feel God's hand on mine. We got to the end of the canoe leg, the first part of the race, and I ran to tag Dr. McCoig, who took off like lightning. He was one of the fastest riders in the state and did eight miles on a mountain bike in twenty-four minutes. I don't remember the runner's name, but he finished with a good time also.

While we were waiting for the winners to be announced, we all enjoyed the big meal provided for us. When the awards were presented, we discovered that we had come in second in our division in a field of seventy-five teams. "Overjoyed" is the only way you could describe Glennie and me. I have always been grateful to Dr. McCoig who gave me this opportunity. I shed tears coming home as I realized I had just participated in a triathlon that was my first real competition since the accident. I felt almost whole again. I thanked God for allowing me to experience this beginning of a new and exciting chapter in my life. I didn't know at the time, but I am sure God did, that this fulfilling event would greatly change my life for the better.

I had been running triathlons with Dr. McCoig's team for about two years, when one day in late March, my friend Glennie and I were training for another Great Greenbrier River Race triathlon. I went home one afternoon after training and was talking to Mom. She said she would like to be in the canoeing part of the race, so I started talking seriously to her about it. Then she said she was just joking. After about a week, I asked her again. At that time she agreed and had contacted two other women who would be a part of her team; however, she still needed a runner. I got in touch with Carol Corson who was the biker on Mom's team to see if she had a suggestion. She said her daughter Rebecca could run, so the team was complete with Mom and Kathy canoeing, Carol bicycling, and Rebecca running.

While the women were training for the race, Glennie and I were both getting into good shape, the best I had been since the accident. We were looking for a bicyclist and a runner. Dr. McCoig called me and gave me the name of Carl Berggerman who agreed to do both events. Glennie and I, as true rednecks, were apprehensive about having someone we didn't know do two-thirds of the triathlon.

About a week before the race, Mom and Kathy started training in canoeing. I took them up to Douthat Lake and showed them everything they needed to know about canoeing. After much practice, they seemed in control. Carol and her daughter had both been in training, so by the end of April, we felt both teams were ready, except for not knowing anything about Carl, and off to the contest we went.

The race consisted of four miles canoeing, eight miles bicycling, and three miles running. The girls were pumped up for the competition, but Glennie and I were still concerned about Carl's participation in two events. We had lots of fans supporting us at the race. The gun went off, one person raced to the canoe that the other person was already seated in, and the race began. When Glennie pushed the canoe into the water, he shoved it so hard that it knocked me down in the boat. He was paddling like mad as I struggled to sit up, and the canoe turned over. There went our chance of winning. Besides, the water had melted from Snowshoe Ski Resort, and it was icy. We dumped the water out of the canoe and got going again, noting that Mom and her partner were still far behind, and this was just the beginning of the race. Glennie and I were freezing but made it up to tag the biker.

Carl, whom we had earlier doubted, took off like a bat out of Hell. Glennie and I stood there dumbfounded for a few minutes until I gathered myself together enough to go to the bridge to check on Mom. She and her partner were coming in second from last. I was proud of them for just staying the course and finishing their leg of the race. They tagged Carol who rode off quickly on her bike, and she and her daughter made up some of the lost time.

After Carl got off the bike, he ran like a rabbit. He finished the race with the best time in both of the events in which he participated. If Glennie hadn't turned over, we would probably have come in first because, even with the mishap, we came in a strong second. Here we had spent all our time worrying about Carl's credentials, and we were the ones who goofed up. Go figure!

Mom and her team finished the race and were proud beyond measure of what they had been able to do. Without the pressure to win, they were able to relax and enjoy the spring day in the presence of family and friends. It was especially nice that Rebecca had come home from Raleigh to be with her mother and that Carol's husband was supporting from the sidelines. It was a great day to be outdoors doing something so thrilling, truly an event to remember. With true professionals alongside, Carol loved doing her best on her rented bike, blending in beautifully with the other athletes who seemed as one with their bikes.

In February of 2004, I decided to compete as an Iron man in the Great Greenbrier Race and do all three segments by myself for the first time. With all the activity I engaged in, I thought I was physically fit. I played basketball once a week in the winter and hiked over mountains all the time. However, I almost died the first time I tried to ride a bike. After the first mile, my quads gave out and I had spaghetti legs. I continued on another mile before I quit, and the next day I could hardly move. Then I tried running, and I was an awkward sight with movements far from fluid, but I was determined to overcome my weakness and be a good runner.

After that first attempt, I thought I was not going to be able to get out of bed the next morning. I hurt all over and couldn't believe I felt this much pain from running a mere two hundred yards! Through pure determination and torture,

I got to the point of riding eight miles on a flat surface and running three miles. This was one of the hardest things I had ever done in my life, almost as hard as the days following my stroke. I guess my being young at the time of my stroke had been helpful as I learned to tie my shoes, walk, talk, ride a bike, and all that follows in relearning. Now, as a mature adult, I tried hard every day to regain some measure of normalcy in my life and not give in to self-pity. Although my personal slogan of "Try Hard" had not been verbalized before this time, it was created during the agony of these days.

My friend Dale agreed to enter the race also, so we started training every weekend starting the first of March to be ready to compete at the end of April. From my brother-in-law, I borrowed a dirt bike weighing 35-40 pounds. Later I found it was one of the heaviest bikes in the race—not a good thing! On the day of the race, Dale's father rode over with us. The kayak I had borrowed from friends was only ten feet long. At the time I didn't know that longer was better.

We prayed right before the race. The first event was the kayak, and we made it through that just fine. In the bike event that followed, I was pedaling my bike like crazy but getting nowhere. Everyone was passing me by, but they were hardly pedaling. I knew then that if I continued to compete in triathlons I needed better equipment. Dale and I both finally made it through the eight miles of biking. By the time I got to the run, I felt more like walking. I forced myself to run even though I had a limp. When I finally made it through, Dale was at the finish line waiting for me. He and his dad both complemented me for completing my first Iron man contest, something I never thought I would do in a million years.

Many articles have been written about my competitions, but one I have kept appeared on August 5, 2005, in the <u>Virginian Review</u>, my local paper published in Covington, Virginia. The article under Josh Hagy's byline carries the headline: "Simpson Sets Record, Wins Gold," and begins with the questions, "What's better than winning a gold medal in the Virginia Commonwealth Games? How about setting a course record in the process?" Virginia Prosthetics, which sponsored me in the kayak race, had equipped me with a brace to hold my hand straight so I could hang on to the oar. I could not have managed without it. I competed against twenty other kayakers on Smith Mountain Lake and surprised myself and the race officials by winning in spite of my handicapping condition. When I saw that six of the competitors had sea kayaks with rudders and additional length which would give them more speed, I knew I would come in behind them. Then I got lost and watched a guy pass me. In the end I was able to rally and edge out the nearest competitor by a full minute. It was a proud moment in my life.

CHAPTER XI
Growing As a Competitor

Carl Berggeman, who had become a good friend, had told me a lot about triathlons in the Berkshire Mountains of Massachusetts. I passed this information on to another friend, Randy, and his response was, "Let's enter!" I enthusiastically agreed. Now let me explain that something happened to me prior to this race. My brother-in-law Ray, who owns a physical therapy shop, was running with me one night. He asked me if I had ever thought about getting a brace. I told him I didn't want anyone to know I was handicapped. Looking back, I don't know how he kept from laughing.

One day not long after this conversation, I was running alone down at the Green Hole and fell because my weak leg dragged. When I tried to get up several times, intense pain kept me on the ground. After lying there an hour with ants crawling all over me, I saw buzzards circling over me. It was a steamy hot day, and I was miserable. Nobody was going to find me in that desolate place. It was a beautiful location along the Cowpasture River, perfect for running because nobody ever came along that way. It was not, however, the ideal place to have an accident. Finally, after two and a half hours, my cousin happened along in his car and wanted to take me to the hospital. Of course, I refused, thinking it was only a hamstring I had injured. This was in June right after the first triathlon I had run as a solo contender in April of this year. When I insisted, he took me home instead of to the hospital and helped me into the house.

After four miserable days, I called another cousin, Shane, for help. I chose him because he was 6 feet, 4 inches and weighed in at 210 pounds. I stood behind him and put my arms around his neck for the trip out to his car. At Dr. McCoig's office, I was examined and x-rayed. His face told me that the news was all bad. He said, "Keith, you have broken your ball joint in two places and have cracked your pelvis."

During the week I spent at the hospital, I had a steady stream of visitors, sometimes fifty in a day. This constant flow of friends and family made me feel good about myself and confident about participating in the triathlon. After leaving the hospital, I used a walker for about four weeks, lost about fifteen pounds, and then resumed training slowly. I was told it would take five months for the hip to heal, but it only took two.

In this also, God was working in my life to lead me toward getting a brace that would keep my toe from dropping and help prevent falls. Although I was fitted right away,

I was told the brace would not be ready for several months, so it would be no help in the Massachusetts race. I should have listened to Ray that evening he first suggested a brace; it is indeed true that "we live and learn."

While the technician at Virginia Prosthetics was fitting me for a brace, I asked if his company would consider sponsoring me in triathlons. The man went back to his boss who agreed to provide whatever I needed. This step revolutionized my ability to compete. This was welcome news, but the Massachusetts triathlon by this time was only a week away, so I had to manage this one on my own.

Prior to the race, I looked around in a junk pile and found a bike. It was an old Raleigh bike that I had ridden fifteen years before the time that I found it. Randy Dolin and I fixed it up and made it useable. He completely replaced the cable, handlebars, tires, and tubes with new equipment. When he took off the pedals, bearings flew everywhere in the gravel. After wasting three and a half hours looking for them, we wised up and took a magnet to locate the little bearings. Thankfully, this method worked. After a week we finally had the bike in running order.

After we solved the bike problem, Randy and I each had to borrow a kayak. By the time September 15 rolled around, we were packed and ready to depart. We made out first stop in Scranton, Pennsylvania, where we spent the night. We drove the entire way in a hard rain. The parking lot of the motel was under six inches of water, and the rain showed no sign of letting up. The next morning we saw on TV that it had rained another five inches that night.

As we continued our trip and neared New York, we looked down a ridge and saw buses parked by a creek that had become a river about a hundred yards wide. It had engulfed thirty of the forty school buses. With heavy hearts, we thought there would be no triathlon, but we continued on with the idea that we had come too far to go back. We made it to Lenox, Massachusetts, and stayed with Gene Peters, an old friend of mine who lived close to the start of the race. He gave us a tour of the entire race course, the Josh Billings Run-A-Ground, a triathlon held at Stockbridge Bowl, a very wealthy area. The race consisted of 28.5 miles road biking, 5 miles kayaking, and 6.5 miles running. We were matched against professionals who had the equipment to show that we were not in their league. Although we stood out like two sore thumbs, we couldn't have cared less.

When we woke up the next morning, the wind was blowing about fifty miles an hour, and rain was falling in sheets. Ivan the Terrible, a hurricane that had followed us from Virginia to Massachusetts had just arrived. Gene took the bikes to the starting point and left the kayaks in his truck at the point where we would begin that part of the race. By the time we began, the wind had slowed to 35-40 miles an hour, and the rain had almost stopped. We started off biking in a group of about 2,500 people. The noise we created was very much like the sound of a freight train. Going downhill, my bike would go only about fifteen miles an hour because of the force of the headwind. I was scared the first time I felt my bike move sideways about half an inch, but I got used to it.

If we thought the kayaking event would be better, we were dead wrong. The breakers on the lake were about two feet high as we started, but at the first turn, the wind whipped up creating breakers three feet high. Because of the height of the breakers, I could not see the kayak next to me. Participants in canoes and kayaks were turning over everywhere. I kept praying, "Please don't let me turn over!" I didn't, thank God. I did all this in a touring kayak that was not meant for the big waves.

The run was next. I started running and met people coming toward me who said I was running the wrong way. I turned around and ran in the direction in which they pointed. I had just ridden 28.5 miles on a fifteen years old bike not made for racing, kayaked 5 miles in 3 foot breakers in a kayak not made for these conditions, and run a half mile in the wrong direction. I was either in a runner's daze or dead tired. While running up a hill, I stepped on a fallen branch, and fell to the ground on my side. I was scared because my hip hurt. It continued to hurt throughout the race, and I prayed, "One step at a time, sweet Jesus." I finished the race seventh from last but was as over-joyed as if I had come in first. I firmly believed that I had trusted in someone greater than myself, one who watched over me every step of the way and gave me strength to finish what I started. Even now, if I fall, which I frequently do, I get right back up and go right on.

It was during this time that Virginia Prosthetics gave me the services of a Public Relations director, Rich Ellis. As I was preparing to compete in a duathlon in Roanoke, Rich arranged for a TV interview. I got a chance to talk about how the brace made by the company had helped me overcome my toe drop as I ran. I did better in this race that I had ever done, maybe because I wanted to do my best to show my appreciation for what the company had done for me.

By March of the following year, I had been in two triathlons and was teaching a Sunday school class of five boys and two girls. I asked them if they would like to work in teams in the Greenbrier River Race, a triathlon which is held every ten years in Greenbrier County, West Virginia. Four boys volunteered to try. I thought they were joking, but they weren't. It was about six weeks until the event, so the boys began training every weekend with me. The church sponsored the group. I asked a boy who was not attending church if he would like to join us, and he said he would like to do an Iron man competition which meant he would run, bike, and kayak on his own. He was only fourteen at the time, but Dairy Queen agreed to sponsor him. The race consisted of three miles running, seven miles biking, and six-and-a-half miles kayaking. My friend Randy and I also competed individually in the race.

On the day of the race, it was raining. Dillon, with the church team, exceeded all expectations in the run; Marcus, his brother, performed well in bicycling even though he had never trained. Matt and Seth canoed and turned over twice, but I was as proud as could be of the whole team. Matt Walton, the fourteen-year-old Iron man, beat me in the run, beat me in the bike race, but lost to me in the kayak competition. He came in second in the teenage division.

Randy stayed ahead of me until I passed him in the kayak with only a mile left. I came in second from last in running, did fair in the biking, but actually did very well in the kayaking, covering 6½ miles in 55 minutes. It was a great time: I came in fourth in my division, Randy came in fifth, and we were all thrilled. Perhaps I, more than anyone else, felt a sense of accomplishment and pride not only for myself but for all the boys who had competed in the race.

In the summer of 2005, I was still participating in triathlons, but something was holding me back, and I didn't know what it was. One day at home, I had just finished brushing my teeth and was walking out of the bathroom when I passed out. Then about four weeks later, I passed out in my living room. Soon I started having headaches, and was light headed. I finished up the triathlons in late fall. One morning while working on my computer, I was entering my name, address, social security number, and related data. Suddenly I could not remember any of this information. The frightening mental block lasted about two hours.

After this incident, my girlfriend, Peg, insisted that I see a doctor who set me up for a sonogram. The technician doing the test told me he could not find my carotid artery. He finally located it but noted that there was no blood going through it. He called a nurse who verified his finding. "You must be a miracle child," was her response. She alerted the doctor who said that the artery on the left side was completely blocked, putting me in an excellent position for having a stroke. All this time I was thinking to myself, "Why me, Lord? Haven't I been through enough?"

The doctor referred me to a vascular surgeon in Roanoke who read the sonogram and said that the carotid artery had probably collapsed within three years after the accident. The blood had rerouted to a place that was not obvious to him but was functioning well. He suggested a heart workup to discover the source of my headaches, light-headedness, and fainting. The next step was seeing a cardiologist who ran an echocardiogram which produced excellent results. He suggested a tilt test to look further for the cause of my problems. Heather, my sister, drove me to Roanoke for that procedure. I was placed on a flat table and tilted upright to a standing position. The doctor said it would take twenty to forty minutes for me to pass out, and he might even have to induce me in order to get the results he wanted. I was thinking this was going to be a long ride, but I passed out in six minutes. The doctor looked at me and said, "Just as I thought!" and asked if I was an athlete. When I replied that I was, he explained that athletes need more sodium than non-athletes. The symptoms I was having were the result of a sodium deficiency.

When I went to see Peg who had been preparing meals for her dad and me, I asked if she cooked with salt. Because of her father's blood pressure and related health problems, she confessed she never added salt to food. She still cooks the same way, but I add salt and drink Gatorade and plenty of water. Since then, the symptoms have cleared up, so again God blessed me. I had been living with blood flow to one side of the brain only, and nobody could explain exactly how the blood was making its way to the right places.

During the 2006 Triathlon season, I was working at Boy's Home and asked Stephen, one of the residents, if he would like to participate. He was interested and, after I explained all the categories, he decided he wanted to be an Iron man. I fixed up a bike for him and borrowed a kayak. Every morning at 6 o'clock, we trained. As we were preparing for the event, I met a minister and a young man who was planning to train for the ministry. They were training for the triathlon also. Of course, my buddy Randy was in it also.

On the morning of the Great Greenbrier River Race, Randy, Steven, and I headed to the race. Steven, at fourteen, was ready for the race; Randy and I shared his anticipation. Our other two new acquaintances showed up later. The race began, and we all finished the run and the kayak event without difficulty. However, three miles into the bike ride, Randy had a flat tire on his road bike from riding on the old gravel railroad bed. The rest of us in my group were riding mountain bikes, not road bikes. Our bikes could handle the gravel better than Randy's. Randy rode his bike for five miles with a flat tire and still managed to finish fifth in his division. Amazing! We all finished the race, and I was especially proud of the boy from the Home. I had told him that, if he set his mind to it, he could finish the race, and he did.

I was ready for another competition and heard that the Lexington Race was a grueling triathlon. The participants had to run up hills, ride up a mountain, kayak down the Maury River, and run again. I found it was really tough! I started out running, thinking I wouldn't do very well, but then I started passing people for the first time in any race. Then I got to the bike leg, passed five people, and was feeling pretty good. In the kayaking segment, I passed about twelve others in kayaks and canoes. At last I finished up with the one-and-a-half mile run and felt positive about myself and my performance. After the race I was invited to lunch at the home of one of the girls who had participated in an all-girls' team. During the meal she handed me the results of the race. I had come in fifth in the Solo Male-Over-Forty category. That was the greatest feeling! I couldn't have felt more thrilled if I had come in first. With my handicap, I had to work four times harder than a person without my physical problems. Fifth place in competition with athletes who had no handicapping conditions was beyond my fondest dream.

CHAPTER XII
Athletes Who Influenced My Life

As I mentioned earlier, I had met Carl Berggeman at a race in West Virginia. We ran into each other again at a triathlon in Lexington, Virginia, where we both competed in the Iron man event. He came in first while I was fifth from last. After the race he came over and complimented me on doing a great job, and I congratulated him on his impressive win. I felt he had commented on my effort because I tried so hard. Then he invited me to join him at a friend's house for dinner, where I met others from the race. In the conversation there, Carl mentioned that he trained a lot at Douthat. When I told him I lived nearby, he suggested that we train together. As we prepared for another race, I discovered he was one of the top athletes on the East Coast.

When Carl trained, he gave 100 percent; when he competed, he appeared to give twice that amount, so I was compelled to step up my training and give a great deal more than I thought I could. I started to improve in all levels with Carl as my motivator. He knew when he could push me harder and constantly encouraged me. He made me feel like a regular guy trying to better myself. For the first time I had someone to teach me how to train in such a way that I built up my endurance by working longer on each segment of the event at each practice session. While he was not obligated to make time to help me, he did. Because he firmly believed in my capabilities, he pushed me to take my self-confidence to a whole new level. I will always be grateful to this wonderful mentor and friend and hope he knows how much I admire and appreciate him.

A very unfortunate event led me to meeting another friend. In the winter of 2004, after my Jeep had rolled over on me, my back hurt me so badly that I could hardly walk. The pain was the result of the injury to two discs that now looked like scrambled eggs. My friend Betty Atkins called to ask me if I would like to go with her sister Peg to a Valentine's Day dance along with Betty and her husband Barry. For a week I bounced ideas around, trying to decide if I felt like going anywhere, much less on a blind date. Betty emphasized that all Peg wanted was a dance partner. I decided to go even though my back pain was killing me. My plan was to survive on pain medication that I would take just before the dance. When I first saw my date, she was wearing a pink sweater with pink fur around the neck and black dress pants. Peg was very pretty, not exactly my type because of her country accent, but could she dance! I made myself dance even though I was in great pain. Peg was completely unaware of my problem. In spite of my extreme discomfort, I enjoyed the evening immensely.

After that initial introduction, we talked on the phone once in a while. We had some informal dates on which we went walking and attended movies. Then, on my birthday in April, we went walking together on Griffith's Knob hunting for mushrooms. We canoed across the river and went halfway up the knob, a really hard walk that led us past my beloved cascading falls. I was thinking that Peg could not handle the walk and would give out along the way, but she didn't. I was the one hurting, and she ended up massaging my back. By the way, we did find some mushrooms. Peg then took me out to dinner to celebrate my birthday, and on the way back we drove through Goshen Pass. From there we drove up on North Mountain on the old road before I took her home and called it a night. After that we started to see each other on a more regular basis. Through our relationship, I met a man I came to admire very much: her father. He amazed me with his ability to solve problems related to mechanics as well as to life situations. Peg comes from a large, loving family just like mine. She lives with her father in the home place, and the other members of the family are in and out regularly.

I am very outdoor-oriented, but I wasn't sure about Peg's interest. However, she surprised me by buying a mountain bike, and we began biking and running together. Soon I was teaching her to paddle a canoe and fish. She is also an avid water skier and skies fifty miles without stopping. Although I cannot keep up with her skiing, we enjoy the lake together.

By August 2005, after Peg had been riding with me for about three months, she decided she was ready to take a long ride and chose the Great Greenbrier River Trail for this adventure. We packed up and left early on a Friday morning. My mom and my uncle took us to the beginning of the ride. The road we had to travel was like one big, long, wiggly snake with room for only one car. I didn't like to think about what we would have to do if we met another car, for there was a bank on one side and a long drop on the other, so Peg and I got on our bikes, and Mom and my uncle wished us luck as they started home.

Other than being humid, it was a glorious morning. We rode through tunnels, saw deer, and met some of the nicest people. At Marlinton, we stopped to rest and pick up one very heavy backpack that we had left there earlier The pack probably weighed about seventy pounds and took all the strength little Peg and I had to hoist it on my back. I got on my bike, started to pedal, and—in slow motion—leaned to the left and kept going, all the way to the ground! Peg couldn't believe what she had just seen. After making sure I was okay, she just about wet her pants laughing. She would have given anything to have videoed my fall for America's Funniest Videos.

After this incident Peg wasn't too sure about the trip or the decision to take the backpack. Anyway, she helped me and the backpack back onto my bike, and off we went. About five miles later, we stopped for lunch. It occurred to me that one way to lighten the backpack was to get rid of the food, so I ate just about everything I could get my hands on, and that was a lot.

Then we pedaled on. The bed and breakfast where we were to spend the night was near the halfway point of our trip, about thirty-five miles from our destination. When we arrived and got off our bikes, the owner said she had not seen a backpack on a bicyclist in five years and that this one we had was probably the biggest and heaviest one she had ever seen. We readily agreed that ours was much too heavy. She suggested we should have bags on the bikes to carry our load. I had never heard before that there was such a thing.

That night as we ate again to lighten our load, humming birds began flying around our heads like little airplanes. We could actually hear them zooming here and there; there must have been hundreds of them. Peg and I loved watching them.

The next morning, with a much lighter load, we began the second half of our trip. After seeing more beautiful sights and wild animals, we were within five miles of the end when lightning (a lot of it), thunder, and hard rain came all at once. We were pedaling through 4 inches of water on the trail. We could not see because of the rain beating on our faces, and we were scared to death that we were going to get struck by lightening. As we pedaled up to the truck, the storm stopped, and the sun came out.

Peg and I dried off, changed clothes, and—realizing we were very hungry—went to a Mexican restaurant to cele-brate. I was so proud of Peg. She was in much better shape at the end of the journey than I. But then, she hadn't carried the backpack either!

Above all, Peg is a caring woman who loves her family and God. She is petite at five feet tall, has blonde hair, a beautiful smile, and a fit body. Her body is like a ball of fire that can do anything, including be as mean as a snake when she wants to be. Deep down in her heart I know there is a pot of gold. Life is good and is falling into place for me.

Where I Am Now

My life is going good. I competed in a one hundred mile bike race, over 14,000 feet elevation gain. This was the toughest one yet. We went nine miles up a mountain. I have to take pills to avoid leg and arm cramps. I brought 14 pills with me. They were all gone half way up the mountain. So, we stopped at the top of the mountain to get some water. The cramps had set in by this time. There was a man there on his bike that had some pills. He gave me 12, which helped me to compete the race. By the grace of God and pure determination, I finished the race. As I crossed the finish line, I was completely worn out, yet joy filled my soul.

I was getting ready to go back to substituting in the schools. A good friend encouraged me to put an application in at the new YMCA as a Health Enhancement Director. I did, thinking I did not have a chance. One interview led to two and to my complete surprise I was blessed with this wonderful job.

We have a brand new beautiful Y. I've learned so much. While there are a lot of responsibilities, I have a lot of fun, too. Four co-workers and family members trained and participated in the Great Greenbrier River Race. I participated with a young man who is autistic and one of my best friends, the most enthusiastic person I have ever met. When we all finished, I was so proud, I felt like crying. They all had just achieved something that they thought was out of their reach. My partner and I came in first in the Challenge Division. I was pleased; my partner was ecstatic.

God never ceases to amaze me. A friend of mine had to move out of state for a job. They asked me to live in a home, on their property as a caretaker. I now live on the beautiful Cowpasture River, in the exact spot where I was baptized as a child. I now have a Blood Hound puppy, a gift, which is my favorite kind of dog. How much better can it get?

Thank you, Dear Lord, for blessing this child of yours. I will always give you Praise and Glory.

EPILOGUE

In looking back over my life, I can now see that drugs and alcohol made my life go steadily downhill. When I got into a hole I couldn't get out of, God's spirit came to me. He had taken from me everything I had depended on to show me that, with his help, I could overcome problems and could share my triumph with those of you who might be struggling with burdens of your own, regardless of what that struggle might be. This book is dedicated to each of you with the hope that you will enjoy reading my story and be encouraged by my account of the power of God working in me. God knows you and sees your pain. If you believe in him, he will refresh your life. He cares, he loves, and he forgives. In whatever circumstance life may throw your way, try hard! Don't ever give up! Take as your motto these words from the New Testament, "I can do all things through Christ who strengthens me."

During the past three years, I have competed in seventeen triathlons, completing all of them. I never quit. I am still tall and slender and sometimes wear a sky-blue pullover that matches the color of my eyes. I have less hair now but still wear the same aftershave. After all I have been through, I am prouder of myself at this stage of my life than I was when I was fourteen.

Before my second attempt in the Josh Billings Run-A-Ground, a television station in Roanoke contacted me for an interview. First, we went to the scene of the car wreck that had started my problems, and the crew ran some footage recounting my injuries and some of my medical history, including my stroke. Then they returned to my house and filmed me from the back of their van while I rode my bike behind it. I thought that was pretty cool. After finishing my segment, they asked to interview my mother. At first she hesitated but finally agreed to talk with them on camera. As she answered their questions, she paid me a very high compliment. She said, "Keith has never blamed anybody for what happened to him in the wreck." I will cherish that comment forever and a day.